I0055465

PRAISE FOR

# GROW GLOBAL

"Today's technologies are *global*, but this book guides you to build the thousand unique *local* relationships for a winning global business. *Grow Global* is a great guide for business leaders everywhere! "
—Marty Zwilling, Founder/CEO, Startup Professionals, Inc., and author, *Do You Have What It Takes to Be an Entrepreneur?*

"I like the content and advice in *Grow Global*. It's solid and practical."
—Don Gabor, speaker and author of *How to Start a Conversation and Make Friends*

"*Grow Global* is a practical guide that everyone needs to succeed in the global marketplace. Jan Yager coaches readers through negotiation, etiquette, contracts and even international virtual communication."
—Diane DiResta, speaker and author of *Knockout Presentations*

"Making a deal happen through business protocol is more important than ever. This very helpful book is a guide for all willing to go global."
—Kanak kr Jain, CEO, Suskan Consultants Private Ltd, Kolkata, India

"As more and more companies look to expand their business, *Grow Global* should be mandatory reading for anyone who will have contact with potential business contacts in foreign countries."
—Ann E. Zaslow-Rethaber, President, International Search Consultants

"After many years in international business, it has become evident that sales are based on trust and for trust to happen, there is a need for understanding. *Grow Global* is a very good and very interesting user-friendly guide to help companies build the cross-cultural understanding that is required for trust in cross-border trade."

—Abdul Rani Achmed, CEO, CWorks Systems.
Malaysia, USA, and Australia

"Wow, I wish I had this book 20 years ago! *Grow Global* provides a comprehensive guide for building business relationships to grow your business internationally. Not only does it include protocols, considerations and the use of social networking, it also includes specific notes on what to do on a country-by-country basis. This book will help guide you through the global growth minefield."

—Phillip Slater, international management consultant and author,
*Smart Inventory Solutions*

# GROW GLOBAL

## SELECTED OTHER BOOKS BY JAN YAGER, PH.D.

### NONFICTION

*Business Protocol: How to Survive & Succeed in Business*
*Productive Relationships: 57 Strategies for Building Stronger Business Connections*
*Who's That Sitting at My Desk?: Workship, Friendship, or Foe?*
*Effective Business and Nonfiction Writing*
*When Friendship Hurts*
*Friendshifts: The Power of Friendship and How It Shapes Our Lives*
*Work Less, Do More: The 14-Day Productivity Makeover*
*Creative Time Management for the New Millennium*
*Creative Time Management*
*365 Daily Affirmations for Time Management*
*365 Daily Affirmations for Happiness*
*365 Daily Affirmations for Creative Weight Management*
*125 Ways to Meet the Love of Your Life*
*Single in America*
*Road Signs on Life's Journey*
*Victims*
*The Help Book*
*Career Opportunities in the Film Industry, 2nd ed* (with Fred Yager)
*Career Opportunities in the Publishing Industry, 2nd ed* (with Fred Yager)

### FICTION

*The Pretty One*
*Untimely Death* (with Fred Yager)
*Just Your Everyday People* (with Fred Yager)
*The Healing Power of Creative Mourning: Poems* (contributor)
*The Cantaloupe Cat* (illustrated by Mitzi Lyman)

# GROW GLOBAL

## Using International Protocol to Expand Your Business **Worldwide**

## Jan Yager, Ph.D.

HANNACROIX CREEK BOOKS, INC.
Stamford, Connecticut

ISBN (13 digit) 978-1-889262-21-5 (hardcover)
ISBN (10 digit) 1-889262-21-8 (hardcover)
Published by:
Hannacroix Creek Books, Inc.
1127 High Ridge Road, #110 Stamford, Connecticut 06905 USA
http://www.hannacroixcreekbooks.com
hannacroix@aol.com

Library of Congress Cataloging-in-Publication Data

Yager, Jan, 1948-
 Grow global : using international protocol to expand your business worldwide / Jan Yager.
    p. cm.
 Includes bibliographical references and index.
 ISBN 978-1-889262-21-5
 1. Business etiquette. 2. Business entertaining. I. Title.
 HF5389.Y344 2011
 395.5'2--dc22
                        2010044788

*This book is dedicated to my family as well as to my colleagues and friends, at home and around the world*

# CONTENTS

# CHAPTER 1

# *Going Global*

It was in the 1980s when I first heard my husband use the word "glocal" in reference to a new strategy being implemented at the financial management firm where he worked to improve the company's chances of growing its business internationally. The word was a combination of the phrases "think globally" but "act locally." And, as within many Fortune 500 companies and other large multi-national corporations, the employees tasked with cross-border interactions were urged to do just that by developing a deep understanding of local cultures, customs, languages and behaviors in order to build stronger business relationships.

Since then, those of us who do business internationally on a regular basis have learned to revise that strategy slightly from "act locally" to "act yourself" while recognizing that certain cultural differences will shape your behavior or attitude. What this means is that going overboard trying to "be" like those in or from the country you are doing business with could backfire.

William Melton is a New York-based lawyer for the software industry who spent fifteen years working for multinational corporations and living in countries including the United Kingdom, the Netherlands, Japan, and Singapore. A Japanese businessman once told him that he liked doing business with Americans because they were very clear and straightforward in what they wanted. But when Americans would visit him in Japan, he continued, they would try to behave like the Japanese and they just looked foolish.

In a related instance, a senior executive shared with me how he was seeking a job with a Japanese multi-national corporation and, in preparation for his interview, he read a number of books about Japanese protocol and behavior. Afterward, he was told by the recruiter that he didn't get the job because he seemed too formal, somewhat introverted and overly deferential—ironically those were the traits the job candidate had decided to emulate because that was what he learned from his readings supposedly typified Japanese business people.. However, this major Japanese company was actually looking for someone to head their American office and wanted a candidate who would be more outgoing, enthusiastic, high-spirited and passionate, or, in other words, someone "more American."

The key is to *know* local customs and behaviors but to still "be yourself" without doing those things that might be offensive to your international business partners. "It's okay to be an American," says Melton, "but you should be polite and respectful and you should listen *without* interrupting, since interrupting is something Americans tend to do a lot. And you should not be *too* informal."

It is an economic necessity that businesses, from the one-person consultancy to the largest major corporation, need to "grow global" or "go global" in order to survive. With manufacturing costs going up and profit margins going down, it is the rare business that can sustain itself without outsourcing some or all of its production to other countries with less expensive work forces or exporting its goods to other markets whose economies may be growing faster or who have a greater need for their products.

A good example is the publishing industry. Publishing companies used to refer to any foreign sales as "found money"—a nice addition to their annual revenue stream but not intrinsically significant. Today, however, with the U.S. book market over-crowded with titles and with profit margins in the publishing industry growing narrower by the minute, I have seen from my own experiences as well as what agents, publishers, and authors are telling me that a growing percentage—for some, more than half—of their revenue is from foreign deals.

It's not just companies with a range of goods to sell or licenses to offer that are looking toward expanding internationally. With unemployment a lingering concern in the U.S., some people are being forced to relocate internationally and take jobs in other countries. Being an "expat" has had status and intrigue associated with it but the "new" expats are often doing it out of necessity, not for a more long-term corporate or career advancement strategy. One couple I know moved to Australia because the husband was having a hard time finding a job in New York. Learning how to fit in with their new culture was one of their first and ongoing challenges as well as adjusting to how infrequently their family or friends were going to make a trip to visit them because of the cost and time involved. Language was occasionally a barrier—if someone spoke too quickly, even if everyone was speaking English, they would have a hard time deciphering some of the words.

As someone who has been doing business internationally for more than three decades, I can attest that "going global" is the easier part. "Knowing local," however, presents many challenges and requires extensive research into those countries where you seek to do business whether by phone, over the Internet, or in person. A simple gesture of greeting in one country could be offensive in another and possibly threaten your chances of doing any business before a conversation even begins.

*Grow Global* is aimed at helping you to avoid the potential minefields that await you as you travel outside the United States to work, as you expand your business ventures internationally in person or even just through your website. The advice in this book is gathered from a range of individuals and situations so that, hopefully, you will find it relevant whether you work in a corporation or are a self-employed entrepreneur; whether you are in an established business or are just now entering the international scene; whether you are a seasoned corporate employee or a new hire; and whether you cultivate that international business through e-mail, by phone, by hosting overseas business visitors, or through foreign travel.

This book is designed to serve three purposes: to provide a basic understanding of the unique customs, gestures, dress, language, values, and attitudes toward money, ethics, and negotiating styles that you may find in other countries; to provide guidance on how to use this understanding to generate international business and sales or, if you are working internationally, how to adapt to any new culture faster so you can get your job done; and to help those who will be doing business internationally from their desk, never leaving for foreign places but talking on the phone, over Skype, or sending e-mails over the Internet.

Most books that discuss international protocol are written with the assumption that the reader is going to be physically traveling to that country, whether for a business trip or relocation. If you are planning to travel to a foreign country, books and other materials written for the international business traveler note that there are a number of things you need to do to shift your behavior depending on what you know about local cultures and attitudes. You are encouraged to make contacts in those countries and to gain an understanding about their customs. It is generally helpful to learn at least some key phrases in the local language and to carry double-sided business cards where one side has your name, company and title in English and the other side has the same information translated into the language of that country. If you are planning on going to another country to cultivate business, or you are moving abroad for your company, you are encouraged to study books or speak with your contacts about how to avoid inadvertently offending someone with a gesture, phrase or attitude. With your upcoming trip, or ex-pat relocation plan on the horizon, you were encouraged to learn to adapt to the ways of conducting business in the country or countries in your line of focus.

Today, however, with the dramatic expansion of the Internet as a global marketplace that is available 24/7 to an ever-increasing number of towns, villages, and cities, the number of users doing business internationally without ever leaving their offices, is staggering. Since 2000, the number of Internet users has grown from an estimated 250 million to 2 billion worldwide, according to the head of the UN's telecommunications agency as reported by AFP news agency (Agence France-Presse) in Yahoo!® News. Those Internet users represent millions upon millions who are conducting business without ever leaving their home whether by e-mail or by placing international phone calls, or video calls, over Skype or other services. Therefore, I've devoted an entire chapter to those virtual travelers who understand the necessity and sensitivity surrounding international protocol and who want to learn more and thrive in this fascinating, expanding source of business opportunities.

I was reminded recently of the challenges of doing business internationally by phone: I decided to call a man in Dubai with whom I had been trading e-mails as we discussed the possibility of my conducting a series of seminars there through his event company. I had hoped that speaking by phone would move our business relationship along. Instead, it pointed out several cultural differences. First of all, I called on a Friday which, he was quick to point out, is always a holiday in any Muslim country. In our phone call, he shared with me that he was originally from India and a Hindu so he was fine with answering the phone and speaking with me. As it turned out, because my potential business partner was Hindu and not Muslim, my *faux pas* of calling on a Friday did not have the irreversible negative impact on our ability to do business together that it might have had.

Second, even though he spoke English, it was extremely difficult to understand what he was saying because of his distinctive accent. Rather than ask him to repeat himself again and again, I asked him to please summarize what we had discussed in our phone conversation in an e-mail. Fortunately, he complied so I could see in writing some of the information he had shared that I could not understand over the phone. Consequently, I decided to go back to communicating with him through e-mail, no longer viewing it as a poor second to phone discussions. However, I am glad I initiated that long-distance phone conversation; the experience pointed out that when I do at some point go to Dubai to conduct seminars, there might be language and custom challenges to consider and deal with—even if everyone in the audience speaks or at least understands English.

Neal R. Goodman, Ph.D. is a sociologist, founder, and president of Global Dynamics, Inc., a company which trains men and women in corporations around the world in what they refer to as "cultural intelligence." Dr. Goodman describes cultural intelligence as "understanding how to leverage the diverse rules of the game of life and business found around the world for competitive advantage." He has a three-step process for increasing your success in doing business globally:

1. Know yourself.
2. Know the other person.
3. Find a middle ground.

"Let's look at the American or western approach to making a decision," explains Dr. Goodman. "Where we like to get a quick decision, we will often deal with people such as Asians who will be quick to say 'yes' when 'yes' does not necessarily mean they are agreeing with you. Sometimes the 'yes' is a respectful way of acknowledging your need. But we interpret this 'yes' as that they want to go forward. Many business relationships have been ruined over something as simple and basic as that. But if you understand this going in, you can get them to say what they really think, maybe not at a business meeting, but later when you go out drinking."

Conversely, assimilating into the U.S. culture can be just as challenging for people from other cultures. A magazine editor in her late 20s had moved the year before to Manhattan from her native London. She recalled that when she first arrived, whenever someone would say to her, "Let's do lunch," she would quickly follow up with a phone call to set up a date for them to go out to lunch together. As her attempts to firm up lunch plans were usually met with resistance, she soon realized that in her new and unfamiliar New York City business world, "let's do lunch" was often a general expression used to designate the end of a meeting, similar to "see you later" or "take care."

You also need to be aware of how attitude plays a key role in each country. Jodi Adams, who runs the Melbourne-based networking business "Corporate Chicks," says, "In Australia people tend to shy away from the 'hard sell.' This would certainly be a relevant point to consider for anyone doing presentations or business in Australia. Australians like to think about purchasing first. The more sales-oriented something is tends to be a negative rather than a positive."

One challenge in writing a book like this is how to view those traits that distinguish one culture from another without making sweeping generalizations or stereotypes. The key is to be aware that although some behaviors are more typical in certain locations or even specific businesses, you cannot assume *everyone* shares in those collective behaviors. Being cognizant of those cultural differences is merely a tool to help you to avoid making a *faux pas*.

For example, you would probably be considered "on time" in Poland as long as you arrive within ten minutes of the appointed time, while in some countries, such as Germany and parts of the United States, some individuals become annoyed if you do not arrive *exactly* at the meeting's start. For instance, I was told about one senior business executive at a major financial services company who would lock the meeting room door at the exact time a meeting was to begin. If you came even a minute late to that meeting, you were locked out.

Just remember as you read *Grow Global* that while certain trends or traits are culture-specific, there are always exceptions. As you get to know people from various cultures, you will learn how he or she is the same or different from grossly over-simplified generalizations.

This book is based on my experiences as a global researcher, writer, and speaker on business protocol and international business as well as someone who has been doing business internationally since my early twenties when I made my first international trips for research, to India and Germany. That experience also includes traveling globally for my position as foreign rights director or consultant for three publishing companies besides my own, with ongoing contact by e-mail, phone, or by meeting at international book fairs with foreign agents or publishers representing more than twenty-eight languages and even more countries than that from around the world.

In addition to my own business and publishing experiences, I did extensive research for my first protocol book *Business Protocol: How to Survive & Succeed in Business,* which has been sold internationally and been translated into several languages including Russian, Vietnamese, Spanish, and Chinese. (A video about business protocol, based on a script I wrote from my book as well as related original written materials that I developed to go with the video, is available for corporate clients through a major online e-learning company Mindleaders.com.)

Over the three years that I researched and wrote *Grow Global*, I have traveled internationally to Asia, Australia, New Zealand, India, the Middle East, and Europe, observing other cultures as well as conducting in-person interviews with businessmen and women who do business globally, as well as with additional protocol experts, many of whom are named in the Acknowledgements section at the end of this book. I also conducted additional interviews by phone as well as communicated via e-mail and reviewed completed surveys to a questionnaire I developed on this topic.

(There are those who I interviewed or communicated with who wished to remain anonymous; their identities are concealed but their contributions to my research are still gratefully noted.)

## WHAT YOU WILL FIND IN THIS BOOK

In Chapter Two, "Understanding the Fundamentals of International Business Protocol," you will find business protocol basics, and international protocol key considerations, ending with two self-evaluation surveys to help determine your current basic and international protocol awareness.

Chapter Three is about building global relationships, the first step in generating international business.

"Rules of the Road: County by Country Etiquette," Chapter Four, provides a sampling of business etiquette concerns in a number of countries.

Chapter Five discusses how to do international business without leaving your office: over the phone, including using Skype, over the Internet, including how to make your website more appealing internationally, as well as tips if you are hosting foreign business visitors.

If you do have to travel for business, Chapter Six provides useful tips for international business travel including suggestions on how to prepare in advance, and how to handle yourself once you arrive so your trip goes as smoothly as possible.

In Chapter Seven, you will learn about topics that come up again and again when you conduct business internationally, namely, gift-giving, ethics, and legal issues such as piracy and copyright infringement.

Chapter Eight covers different negotiating styles you are likely to find in various countries, and Chapter Nine is about Contracts and Getting Paid.

A brief "Summing Up" is the last chapter in this book followed by an appendix, glossary, bibliography, resources, acknowledgements, an index, and about the author.

Whether you are employed by a giant multi-national company, working for yourself or for a small start-up, a lawyer in a large practice or your own firm, a consultant with clients in Europe and Asia, or a manufacturer with a website that you want to turn into a thriving international business, this book is for you. It provides you with the tools necessary to go global, helping you to choose how you want to behave when you are traveling or relocating for business, entertaining visitors from other countries, or how to interact over the phone or over the Internet, in order to successfully grow your business or career beyond the borders of your own country.

# CHAPTER 2

# Understanding the Fundamentals of International Protocol

You've just flown fourteen hours half-way around the world for an important business meeting in Mumbai, India. The traffic from the airport to the downtown office building was horrendous, but you still managed to arrive with a minute to spare. Proud of your punctuality, you enter the room ready to exchange greetings—only to find you are the only one there. The clock on the wall says 8:59 so you settle down as you wait for others to join you for the meeting that had been scheduled to begin at 9 a.m. As the clock ticks, you become more anxious by the minute.

By 9:10 you start to get angry, wondering why the people you hoped to be doing business with were standing you up. You check your Blackberry (or your iPhone). Maybe someone sent you an e-mail about being delayed in traffic? You look at your cell phone for a possible missed call. Did someone cancel the meeting and forget to tell you? What kind of irresponsible behavior is this? Maybe you should reconsider doing business with these people if they can't even get to a meeting on time.

Then, at 9:15, one after another, six men and one woman enter the room, smiling. One by one, they walk over and reach out to shake your hand, acting as if nothing is wrong—when they see the scowl on your face.

"Is something the matter?" one of them asks. You are about to make a comment about how you don't like to be kept waiting when a voice in the back of your head yells, "Stop! Think about where you are. This is Mumbai, India not lower Manhattan!" In India, if you arrive at 9:15 for a 9 a.m. meeting, you are still considered to be on time. In fact, if you had said something critical about their punctuality, which Indians take very seriously, you could have derailed the entire meeting, insulting six people vital to the deal you've been working on through e-mails and phone calls for the last six months. You would have lost any opportunity to establish a relationship with this roomful of potential business partners and customers. Rather than criticize your business associates, you instead shake hands and then bow as you say "*Namaste,*" meaning, "I bow to you."

This is just one example of how an insensitivity to correct business protocol or, more simply put, "not doing the right thing" in different cultures could kill a deal.

Besides meeting start-times, even the speed at which business gets done has wide cultural variations. Someone from the United States, known for its aggressive, frenzied pace, may expect business to be transacted just as swiftly in most other cultures, where the pace may be a lot slower. Making a deal happen in some cultures could take a matter of months or years rather than the days or weeks that Americans generally expect.

The key is to remain patient and accept that it will take however long it takes depending on where the business is being conducted. This attitude will take you a lot further than constantly nagging about a deal taking longer than anticipated. The concepts of time and punctuality are cultural phenomena, and each culture thinks their perspective is the correct one. Taking this to the extreme, when I was in the Fiji Islands, I was told more than once that "Fiji time is no time. You can't be in a rush in Fiji."

## Why Business Protocol is More Important Than Ever

Understanding business protocol has always been important; the Internet has only made it more so. Connections involving potential business deals and relationships that may have once taken days or weeks and multiple phone calls, are now happening at the speed of light over the Internet. The potential for making an inappropriate or offensive misstatement in an e-mail should not be taken lightly. Careers have been destroyed because of it. There's a saying that goes something like this: if someone is pleased with a product or service, they tell one other person; if they are displeased, they tell a dozen. Today, with our addiction to social networking, you can probably multiply that by a 100 or even 1,000. Imagine the "bad press" you or your product could receive if your business interaction is the subject of a negative posting on LinkedIn.com, xing.com, Facebook.com, Twitter.com, and so on.

Also, with most of the world recovering from the worst recession in decades, many countries and businesses are economically challenged. Therefore, it is more likely that if someone has a choice among multiple companies for business and if everything else such as price, convenience, quality, or ability to deliver on time is equal, the respectful use of proper business protocol could determine who gets that business as well as who gets to keep it.

Take this self-evaluation survey to measure your current Business Etiquette Quotient (BEQ).

## Your Business Etiquette Quotient[1]

Pick the answer to each question that accurately reflects what you usually do (not what you *wish* you would do) in the following situations:

1.  When I am invited to a business function, I always RSVP (respond) within the week.

    *a*   *Yes*          *b*   *No*          *c*   *Sometimes*

2.  I always return a phone call the same day I receive a message.

    *a*   *Yes*          *b*   *No*          *c*   *Sometimes*

3.  I never use curse words at work.

    *a*   *Yes*          *b*   *No*          *c*   *Sometimes*

4.  I always write a thank you note, send a thank you e-mail or make a thank you phone call for meals, gifts, or any kind of extra kindness extended to me.

    *a*   *Yes*          *b*   *No*          *c*   *Sometimes*

---

[1] *This self-evaluation is excerpted and reprinted from* Business Protocol *by Jan Yager, Ph.D., with permission of the publisher of the 2nd edition, Hannacroix Creek Books, Inc.*

5. My table manners are exemplary.

   *a*   *Yes*          *b*   *No*          *c*   *Sometimes*


6. I see myself as part of a team, rather than as a lone corporate player mainly seeking praise for my individual efforts.

   *a*   *Yes*          *b*   *No*          *c*   *Sometimes*


7. I answer important letters immediately and take care of the rest of my e-mails or mail within a few days or by the end of week.

   *a*   *Yes*          *b*   *No*          *c*   *Sometimes*


8. Before dealing with someone from another culture, I take the time to find out the proper etiquette unique to that person's culture so I do not unwittingly offend anyone.

   *a*   *Yes*          *b*   *No*          *c*   *Sometimes*


9. I give verbal or written credit where credit is due.

   *a*   *Yes*          *b*   *No*          *c*   *Sometimes*


10. I send holiday cards or appropriate gifts to my most highly valued business relationships.

   *a*   *Yes*          *b*   *No*          *c*   *Sometimes*


Give yourself a 3 for each *yes* or *a* answer; a 2 for each *c* or *sometimes*; and a 1 for each *b* or *no*. Add up your score. If you rated a score of 28-30, your BEQ is excellent. If you got 25-27, you have a good BEQ. If your score is 20-24, your BEQ is fair. If your score is 10-19, you have a poor BEQ. Now reconsider your answers. Pat yourself on the back for each "yes" and make special note of your "no's". Those are just some of the areas you need to work on. Your "sometimes" answers indicate you know the right thing to do, but you need to be more consistent in doing it. The good news is that all ten issues raised in the BEQ self-evaluation are discussed in this book.

Before going on to discuss international protocol, let's address some basic business etiquette behaviors.

## THE SIX BASIC PRINCIPLES OF BUSINESS PROTOCOL

Generally speaking, based on the original extensive research I conducted with more than 200 human resource managers, other protocol experts, and business executives when writing my book *Business Protocol*, and in reviewing those principles over the years since that initial work, there are still six basic protocol principles that apply to most business interactions. Once you are completely comfortable with these, we can move on to how they may vary from culture to culture and country to country.

---

**PRINCIPLE #1**
**BE DISCREET**

---

Being discreet is another way of saying you should maintain confidences and avoid the spreading of gossip or rumors. In some businesses, discretion is not only a business etiquette principle; sharing corporate information can be considered a breach of contract. One example of this would be insider trading, which is punishable by law.

---

**PRINCIPLE #2**
**BE ON TIME**

---

Always be on time, keeping in mind, as noted previously in this chapter, that the concept of being "on time" varies from culture to culture. Still, you need to be "on time" for whatever culture you are in. Being late, whether by fifteen minutes or five, is often considered rude and inconsiderate. You may think being caught in traffic or the fact that your previous meeting ran long would be met with understanding. Not always. You risk the chance that the person with whom you are supposed to meet may only pretend to

14

understand your excuse but in reality he or she is thinking you are a poor planner or that you should have started out sooner. Or worse, you just didn't think this meeting was important enough to arrive on time.

Being on time also applies to phone calls that you have scheduled with an international business associate. Every international business person has a story about waking up his foreign partners or customers in the middle of the night or on a holiday, only to get an earful. It is important to check time and day differences (Asian countries are generally one full day ahead of the U.S.), as well as the definition of "business days and hours" before calling.

Fortunately, there are numerous websites that can help the geographically-challenged figure out what time it is anywhere else in the world.

> www.timeanddate.com

## PRINCIPLE #3
## BE COURTEOUS, PLEASANT, AND POSITIVE

Attitude is, indeed, contagious. Being upbeat at work is not just a good business protocol principle but fundamental to your reputation and image if you want to get ahead in your career or if you would like your department or company to have a better chance at success.

## PRINCIPLE #4
## BE CONCERNED WITH OTHERS, NOT JUST YOURSELF

This principle has become even more vital since social media networking sites have become so pivotal to developing, strengthening, and expanding business connections. You get by giving and this applies to those social networking sites as well. Be careful not to appear too self-absorbed or opportunistic. Showing concern about others and their businesses and companies will take you further than will simply talking about yourself.

## PRINCIPLE #5
## DRESS APPROPRIATELY

You don't wear a tie to a barbecue or shorts to a business meeting (unless it's on the beach or in Hollywood). Dressing appropriately shows respect to those with whom you are meeting. We will be looking at this issue in greater detail when we get into international protocol, but the simplest rule of thumb is to find out if you are expected to wear local native dress or if a business suit is acceptable, especially for a woman who might be traveling to countries that have strict guidelines about appropriate dress for women.

## PRINCIPLE #6
## USE PROPER WRITTEN AND SPOKEN LANGUAGE

Avoid using foul language at work and in business, whether verbally or in writing. This may seem like a "no brainer" but it is a principle that still needs to be emphasized. There are numerous news accounts of former heads of state inappropriately using foul language and nearly sparking international incidents. It is also key to remember that online writings, even those intended for sites that you thought were not related to your work, could come up in "alerts" associated with your name on the Internet. So be extra careful about anything and everything you say in writing online as well as what you say verbally.

Now let's adapt and expand upon those six basic principles into fifteen key international business protocol concerns. Some of those issues are going to seem obvious but you would be surprised at how often the things we take for granted can hit us from behind when we least expect it.

Now take this International Business Etiquette Quotient (IBEQ) that follows.

16

# YOUR INTERNATIONAL BUSINESS ETIQUETTE QUOTIENT

The fifteen questions in this self-evaluation survey and its analysis are geared toward general international protocol concerns, and are not country-specific.

1.  I take the time to figure out how to say or write someone's name in their language as well as assessing the gender of the person with whom I am communicating.

    *a*  *Yes*        *b*  *No*        *c*  *Sometimes*

2.  I consider the proper introduction if I am visiting another country or if someone from another culture is visiting me at my company.

    *a*  *Yes*        *b*  *No*        *c*  *Sometimes*

3.  I consider the business card etiquette in each culture including how to properly offer my card, whether or not it should be imprinted in two languages—in English on the front and in the native language on the back—and I have a business card holder that I place the card into after I have read over the card that I am being offered.

    *a*  *Yes*        *b*  *No*        *c*  *Sometimes*

4.  Dining and eating customs are so culture-specific that I take the time to read about, or conduct informational interviews, on these habits before I visit or host someone from another culture.

    *a*  *Yes*        *b*  *No*        *c*  *Sometimes*

5.  I am well aware of what constitutes punctuality in each of the cultures that I am visiting—not just as it applies to meeting times but also in

terms of the expected pace of any project or work we are doing together.

*a* *Yes*                    *No*                    *Sometimes*

6.  I consider the location of each business meeting and choose a place that is appropriate for that culture or industry.

    *a* *Yes*          *b* *No*          *c* *Sometimes*

7.  I carefully consider who should be in attendance at each meeting, trying hard to avoid offending anyone by including those who are too senior or too junior.

    *a* *Yes*          *b* *No*          *c* *Sometimes*

8.  I take the time to figure out the proper attire for business meetings as well as for any business-related social events.

    *a* *Yes*          *b* *No*          *c* *Sometimes*

9.  Being recognized as someone who uses acceptable written or spoken language in each culture that I do business in is important to me so I take the time to master what I need to know including a few greetings and basic phrases in the native language.

    *a* *Yes*          *b* *No*          *c* *Sometimes*

10. I know that gestures and body language are culture-specific so I am studying those relevant to each culture that I am doing business in so I do not unwittingly misinterpret any gestures or expressions.

    *a* *Yes*          *b* *No*          *c* *Sometimes*

11. I am aware of the standard negotiating style in each culture I am doing business with.

    *a   Yes*          *b   No*          *c   Sometimes*

12. I do my homework and find out what topics or politically incorrect issues I should avoid so I will not offend anyone.

    *a   Yes*          *b   No*          *c   Sometimes*

13. I know where gift-giving and receiving is acceptable and expected, and I also know what guidelines to follow so I will not make gift choices that might be considered influence peddling or that would put me in the position of being accused, however falsely, of taking a bribe.

    *a   Yes*          *b   No*          *c   Sometimes*

14. I make an effort to find out what holidays are celebrated so I am aware of these times when international business colleagues may be unavailable either to receive or answer e-mails or phone calls or to receive me if I happen to be traveling to that country at that time.

    *a   Yes*          *b   No*          *c   Sometimes*

15. I conduct interviews or read about religious practices and related concerns such as dress, eating customs, or holidays for each culture with which I conduct business.

    *a   Yes*          *b   No*          *c   Sometimes*

Give yourself a 3 for each *yes* or *a* answer; a 2 for each *c* or *sometimes* answer; and a 1 for each *b* or *no*.

If you scored 40-45, your international protocol is very good to excellent. You are aware of what concerns you need to address in general and how these apply to each culture or country you are dealing with in a specific way.

If your score is 25-36, take a look at what questions you answered with "sometimes" or "no." Those questions indicate where you need to put your energy and time to get your international protocol skills up to the level that would be advantageous to your career.

If your score is 15-25, you have your work cut out for you. Fortunately, you will find help in the pages that follow as you will learn the fifteen key international protocol issues that you need to master to comfortably grow your business worldwide.

## FIFTEEN INTERNATIONAL PROTOCOL CONSIDERATIONS

### CONSIDERATION #1
### CORRECT PRONUNCIATION AND WRITING OF SOMEONE'S NAME

If there is one thing all humans have in common it is that we like to hear the sound of our own names. Some of us even like to see it in print. But just as much as we like to see or hear our name, we dislike seeing it misspelled or mispronounced. In business, using someone's name is how we personalize that connection. Therefore, it becomes very important not to misspell or mispronounce the name of someone you want to do business with. Equally important is not to make the wrong assumption about someone's gender because of your unfamiliarity with that name in a particular culture. This has become more of a challenge because of e-mail and the Internet.

Obviously if someone attaches a photo with his or her e-mail it will be easier to discern their gender if their name leaves that unclear. But if someone does not include a photo, you can still do a search of names on Google that may give you a clue as to whether the name is masculine or feminine. (There are a few that could be either.)

You could also see if that person has a profile at LinkedIn.com or xing.com, two social networking sites that include photos in their subscribers' bios. You might also find other places on the Internet where that individual is described or depicted; if you have colleagues at that (or at another) company in the same country, you might be able to find out someone's gender without causing offense. Depending upon your relationship with the person you are asking, you could say something as simple as, "I'm communicating with so-and-so and I am unable to tell by the name if it is a male or female. Do you have any idea?"

If you speak on the phone, by landline or Skype, you might of course also learn if someone is a male or female but today, there are business relationships that exist completely through the Internet. Initiating a phone conversation, especially if you and your business colleagues are separated by so many time zones that it is difficult to coordinate speaking, can be a step forward in your business relationship; but, it should be one that happens at the appropriate time and not artificially early because you are trying to determine someone's gender.

Spelling is another protocol concern; check and recheck how you spell someone's name especially if it is a language and culture that you are not familiar with.

## CONSIDERATION #2
## PROPER GREETINGS AND INTRODUCTIONS

The world-renowned business etiquette expert Letitia Baldrige said it best when she wrote that "The way in which you meet others—what you do with your body and your voice—shows the kind of person you are."

That statement is so wise and fundamental. In that initial moment, whether you extend your hand or send an e-mail that is angry or unwittingly inappropriate, you will define who you are to the other person.

I also want to point out that whether or not Baldrige, when she wrote this pre-Internet, was referring to just meeting in person or not, today the concept is just as valid even though we now have to also include "meeting" over the Internet as well as over the phone or through Skype, which increasingly includes a video component to the interaction, not just an auditory one.

Baldrige continues with: "If you meet others with interest, showing good manners, they will respond immediately to you." As the saying goes, you never get a second chance at making a first impression.

Whether or not you should extend your hand for a handshake, or bow, or kiss someone on the cheek is often the very first aspect of international business protocol that you need to address. There's even a book on the subject entitled *Kiss, Bow, or Shake Hands* by Terri Morrison and Wayne A. Conaway (with the original version also by George A. Borden, Ph.D.) It covers what to do in sixty countries and I highly recommend it. (Reference the Bibliography section of this book.)

Knowing how to greet someone is pivotal whether you are a young, entry-level employee traveling to your first trade show in Seoul, Korea, or the President of the United States, traveling half-way around the world to meet Japan's Emperor Akihito—to whom President Obama bowed, to much fanfare and ridicule. As Andrew Malcolm and Johanna Neuman point out in their *Los Angeles Times* blog about President Obama's bow, it might have gotten positive nods from the older generation in Japan, who think their royalty should get such deference from another world leader, but there were Americans who thought that if President Obama had instead shaken the Emperor's hand, it would have been a more appropriate greeting.

Knowing how to greet someone in a business capacity is no small matter. It can set the tone for any international business meeting: awkward or comfortable, strained or acceptable.

What are the most common greetings that you will encounter in international business? Outside of Asia, for men, it will be the handshake; for women, it will also be the handshake, but if there is a friendship between the two women, or they have met in business before, it might be a kiss on one cheek, on both cheeks, or even a three-kiss greeting.

Business etiquette consultant Lydia Ramsey points out that historians trace the handshake back several hundred years to England "as a method to communicate that you were empty-handed and unarmed during a meeting." She notes in her article, "Shaking Hands throughout History and Around the World" that "Most cultures encourage handshaking more often than the United States." Ramsey also points out that in some countries men are not permitted to touch an unrelated woman; in Kuwait, it is considered inappropriate to shake hands with an unrelated female. So if you are a woman traveling for business, check on the handshaking rules for whatever country you are visiting to make sure handshaking between a man and a woman is permissible.

Kissing on one check is less acceptable in business than the handshake but it could also be a question of what type of business you are in. The more conservative businesses like finance or banking tend to lean toward the handshake as the more appropriate way to initiate a business meeting. But the liberal fields, like publishing, fashion, or film, show a preference for the kiss, whether for two women in business or a woman and a man. In the United States, it is usually a single kiss. But internationally, especially in Europe, it would be a double kiss, on one cheek and then the other.

If it is considered appropriate to kiss in business, turn your head to the left to first offer the right cheek. This is a common business greeting in many European countries as well as in other countries around the world, such as Brazil. There may also be distinctive differences between how certain cultures greet in business versus in friendship situations (which also holds true for the United States). In Belgium, for example, where shaking hands is typical at the beginning and end of a business meeting, men and women may "touch cheeks and kiss the air three times, alternating cheeks," according to *Kiss, Bow, or Shake Hands*.

However, for the purpose of breaking into business internationally, just concern yourself with what is expected and required in business. You will learn what is more typical as relationships deepen and extend into the friendship realm with time and experience within each culture.

A secondary consideration is physical space. When meeting in person, each culture has its own standard for how much physical space is expected and comfortable. Brazilians are more likely to stay in close proximity throughout a conversation, as are Mexicans and Italians, whereas the British need a lot of space in their business interactions to feel comfortable.

Probably the most pivotal idea that I want to get across in *Grow Global* is that there is no overarching "right" way to introduce yourself or to greet

*Probably the most pivotal idea that I want to get across in Grow Global is that there is no overarching "right" way to introduce yourself or to greet others. Whether it is "correct" to shakes hands, bow, or kiss on one or both cheeks, depends on the culture in which you find yourself.*

others. Whether it is "correct" to kiss, bow, or shake hands depends on the culture in which you find yourself. Americans may think that shaking hands is "the" way to greet someone in business, but if a woman did that in a country where women are forbidden to touch an unrelated male, that meeting would start off on a very somber note—and possibly not continue at all.

Therefore, knowing the proper way to greet someone is vital for successfully conducting international business. Take for example P.J. McGuire who runs a business protocol training company based in Chicago called Modet, Inc. A company reached out to her to work with one of their employees who had been sent to China along with several other colleagues. This employee, a sales representative in her late twenties, was "a hugger." That means she would greet people in her office by hugging them.

When "the hugger" got to China, she proceeded to hug the people she was meeting for business. She didn't know that you are not supposed to hug people in a business meeting or negotiation in China. McGuire tried to help the woman change what had become a habit but she couldn't. But the situation became so bad that on the last two days of meetings, they had to leave this woman at the hotel because they were afraid she was going to continue hugging everyone. She did it spontaneously. She could not stop herself, to the chagrin of her Chinese counterparts who seemed shocked and offended. (That woman is no longer with that company.)

In general, there is a pecking order of who is introduced to whom when people meet in business. As Baldrige notes in her classic *Complete Guide to Executive Manners:*

- The younger person should be introduced *to* the older person.

- A junior executive is introduced *to* the senior executive.

- Introduce a peer in your own company *to* a peer in another company.

- A nonofficial person should be introduced *to* an official individual.

- Another executive should be introduced *to* a client or customer.

Always use the person's full name, either Bob Smith or Mr. Bob Smith, and not just someone's first name when you are introducing him or her unless you have been given permission to use someone's first name alone. I remember an interview I did with an executive who shared with me the collective "gasp" at the meeting where one of the younger employees referred to him by just his first name in front of the room of employees. The employee was quickly corrected as to the proper way to refer to the head of the company, although the CEO would be showing perfect protocol to refer to the junior employee by his first name alone.

It is also far better, when you are meeting people internationally, to have that person say to you, "You may call me so-and-so," and let them give you permission to call them by just their first name, or a nick name, than having you ask, "May I call you so-and-so?" since that could put them on the spot. A better way would be to simply ask, "How would you like to be introduced?"

---

### CONSIDERATION #3
### THE EXCHANGE OF BUSINESS CARDS

---

It has almost become a cliché to say the Japanese have turned the exchange of business cards into a ritual covering how a card is presented, considered, and stored. But Japan is not the only culture that values the exchange of business cards. Attend a trade show anywhere in the world and you will find yourself exchanging cards with practically everyone you meet. In fact, the only real reminder of your interaction afterwards may be that business card.

Some of the things that the Japanese are concerned about are actually of universal importance. For example, one of the reasons a Japanese person will scrutinize a business card so carefully at the beginning of a meeting is to make sure that he or she is meeting with someone who is at the appropriate level; that they have not been partnered with someone too low at the company, or too high.

The Japanese are not alone in this; most people, when presented with a business card, will ask themselves: who is this person? What is his or her title? On your business card, include your company address, even if you mainly operate a website business, so the person to whom you give your card can figure out where in the world you are based. Phone numbers, if you are doing a global business, should include the complete number, including country code and city code. If you have a separate fax line, list it, once again with complete information. If you are on Skype, include your Skype name. If you want to increase your Twitter followers and presence, you can include that information as well.

Bottom line: if a business card is to facilitate a business interaction, provide all the information that someone would need to easily follow-up with you. Be cautious about filling the card up with too much information that is superfluous.

When doing business internationally with a particular country, put a translation of your business card on the back of your card as a courtesy to your international clients/customers/colleagues.

When you design your card, keep in mind that it can be nice to write a personal note on a card if you are attaching it to printed materials that you are sending to someone. Letitia Baldrige suggests putting a "slash through your name" and then writing something on the front, in pen, or on the back, if there is no room on the front of the card.

When you consider the paper for your cards as well as the design and type font, consider the image you want to project. If you want to show consideration for those in business who have trouble reading very tiny print, try to avoid miniscule writing on the card, even for your address.

Who you give your business card to is as pivotal as when you give it out. If you are having a business meeting with someone, it is fine to exchange cards at the beginning of your meeting. You have to be careful if you are at a business function, like a networking event or a cocktail party, not to give out your card to anyone and everyone that you meet. It will look as if you are indiscriminate about who gets your card, which will diminish you in the eyes of those with whom you do have a business relationship, or a new contact with whom you hope to develop a connection.

Certainly keep your cards clean and appealing. Expect to get oversized cards in Europe that will not easily fit into a typical business card holder. Avoid letting your business colleague see you folding or bending an oversized business card to fit it into your holder. Instead, place it unfolded inside of your notepad.

## CONSIDERATION #4
## DINING AND EATING CUSTOMS

Being polite about the food you are offered when you are traveling internationally for business is sometimes quite challenging. For example, when Gayle Carson, a Florida-based speaker and author, was in Indonesia, her host invited Gayle and her husband to eat lunch with him over the weekend. Says Gayle: "We went to a mountain town and he ordered for us. When the appetizer arrived, it was supposed to be their greatest delicacy. It turned out to be a full bird complete with eyes, feet, and all the rest. I pushed it around my plate until he left to make a phone call and then called the waiter to remove it."

In some countries such as India, find out if your host is vegetarian before ordering meat, which he or she could find offensive.

## CONSIDERATION #5
## PUNCTUALITY

It has already been mentioned that what constitutes "being on time" varies widely from culture to culture. It is important to know what is common with whatever culture or country you are dealing with. If being "on time" in a certain culture means being ten minutes late, then by showing up exactly on time, you may find that your host is unprepared to greet you because you are actually considered "early" and somewhat rude because you violated the "ten minutes late means on time" rule for that culture.

## CONSIDERATION #6
## MEETING CONCERNS: LOCATION

Each culture is unique about where a business meeting will take place: it could be in the executive's office, in a conference room or lobby of a five-star hotel, at a restaurant, or at the host's home.

For international meetings, remember that if you suggest a dinner or a lunch at a restaurant, you are usually expected to pick up the tab. So invite with that in mind, not only who you are inviting but at what restaurant the meal will occur. (And make sure you pick a restaurant that will either take your credit or debit card or that you have enough cash to pay for the meal if the establishment is "cash only" and so save yourself from embarrassment.)

---

### CONSIDERATION #7
### WHO WILL ATTEND THE MEETING?

---

In India, don't be surprised or offended if your host has invited his or her parents to the business meeting. This is considered an honor.

Dr. Rachna Kumar, Program Director, Business and Management Programs at Alliant International University in San Diego, California and international business consultant, described to me how important hierarchy is in China in terms of who will be at a meeting. Says Dr. Kumar: "They are very rigid about the reporting hierarchy and who would be at a meeting and the title of the people at the meeting. They were very conscious of the fact that if you are a manager, you meet a manager and they will identify who is at the same level. When you go to the meeting, you expect to find your counterpart and sit directly across from the person who is your counterpart and you don't talk across lines. The flow of conversation is almost one by one. One person speaks and hands over to the next hierarchically obvious person to speak. It is a back and forth conversation but it is not a discussion. You almost take turns at speaking. Now it is your turn to speak."

---

### CONSIDERATION #8
### PROPER DRESS

---

When I was 23, I traveled to India to research my first book on the history of vegetarianism. It was at a time that mini-skirts were popular in the United States so I wore a suit with a mini-skirt. Soon after arriving, I had to travel by motorcycle and my mini-skirt rode up on my thighs. I caused quite the negative reaction as we drove through the crowded streets of New Delhi at lunchtime as businessmen all dressed in suits were taking their mealtime break. I quickly got the hint, bought a *sari*, learned how to drape it, and wore *saris* the rest of the month of my business trip. At that time, more than thirty years ago, blending in helped me to conduct interviews, and to travel more comfortably in cities and even rural areas. I did, however, have to be accompanied by another woman or a man. Back then, a business woman was not supposed to travel or even walk alone in India.

More recently, upon finalizing a discussion with the meeting planner who was inviting me to Kolkata, India, I asked him if it would be appropriate to wear a business suit or if I should wear a *sari*. He replied that a business suit would be fine for the presentation but they were having a gala dinner that evening, and said I could wear a *sari* then if I wanted to.

The key to remember about proper dress is to find out how the people you are meeting with are dressed and then, if possible, to dress in a similar fashion. If not, a business suit generally is acceptable. When in doubt, just ask.

---

### CONSIDERATION #9
### ACCEPTABLE WRITTEN OR SPOKEN LANGUAGE
### WRITTEN LANGUAGE

---

Today, more than ever before, acceptable writing applies to e-mails as readily as it does to formal business letters. Knowledge of traditional business correspondence is still required. In my book, *Effective Business and Nonfiction Writing*, I devote many chapters to the basics of writing clear and acceptable writing for business. In a nutshell, what you write has to be:

- Clear in thought and facts.

- Correct in terms of grammar and spelling.

- In a tone that is appropriate for the type of communication and the relationship you have with the recipient of your communication, e.g., not too friendly or effusive, and yet not too abrupt, distant, or cold.

- Responsive to whatever information is being requested whether it is a confirmation for a meeting or a reaction to a submission.

## SPOKEN LANGUAGE

Even if English is becoming a universal language for conducting business internationally, there are still countries where business is conducted in the native language—especially if you venture outside the major, larger cities into the towns or rural communities. It may be unrealistic to learn the entire native language in advance of a business trip that will only last two weeks, but you can at least learn a couple of key expressions in the local language to help break the ice.

If you are going to be doing business with a country but are not fluent in that language, you can hire an interpreter or a translator to accompany you to key business meetings. You could also ask a colleague at your firm to join you on the trip if he or she speaks that language fluently.

If you are doing business via the Internet, make sure that contracts and important business documents are always presented to you in both English and the native language rather than just in a language you are unable to read yourself. If you are worried that the person helping you with the contract does not have your best interests at heart, you can always hire your own translator to read both versions of the contract, comparing the original to the English version, making sure that the translation is accurate.

Melinda Bates, who ran the White House Visitors Office in the late 1990s, shared with me a very telling anecdote that she also wrote about in her book, *White House Story*. It emphasized how understanding the meaning of a word in a certain culture can make or potentially break an international situation and relationship. As Bates explains:

> The President and Mrs. Clinton had decided to welcome the Chinese president and we were heavily into the planning. We'd done many of these events so no one had any real concerns except [that] the state dining room, although large by American standards, is not large enough for some state dinners. It can only seat 130 guests, not nearly enough room to take care of the 400 guests that they wanted to invite.

We decided the only solution was to set up a tent on the South Lawn of the White House....When I say 'tent' you may have a mental image of some large tent that you've seen somewhere. Forget it. You've never seen a tent like this. Size-wise, think 'airplane hangar' and you've got an idea. As to what it looked like, well, somehow it stands without internal supports. So it's a big empty canvas to decorate. Glittering chandeliers hanging from the ceiling, trellises with flowering plants ornament the sides, making it look like a garden space. A famous decorator, David Tutera, set up panels painted to look like the inside of the East Room. Lighting made the space feel intimate. It was so magical that people said "ooh!" when they stepped inside.

So what's the problem? Well, we're moving ahead, not dreaming there's any problem until the State Department tells the Chinese the State Dinner will be held in a tent. We think they'll be pleased to know how many people want to come. No, they're not. It turns out that to the Chinese, the word *tent* is associated with disasters. As in "the villagers were sheltered in tents after the flood." "Is it the structure they care about or is it the word itself?" I asked.

"We think it may be just the word."

"Okay then. How about we still put up the same structure but we call it a *pavilion*?"

Well, *pavilion* is a happy word to the Chinese, so there were smiles all around, we got to invite our 400 guests and the simple change of a word saved the day.

---

## CONSIDERATION #10
## GESTURES AND BODY LANGUAGE

---

A gesture such as beckoning someone by waving a curled finger is considered condescending and insulting in India. Roger Axtell has made a career out of advising others about international customs in his enormously popular *Do's & Taboos* series of books. He shares the story about the Saudi Arabian distributor who suddenly grabbed his hand and continued walking down the street, swinging his hand. Axtell later found out that his Saudi host was showing him a sign of respect and admiration by walking down the street, swinging their hands. "If I had pulled away it would have been a terrible insult," Axtell explains.

Unless you live in another country for a period of time, it is unrealistic to try to learn all the gestures that depict a particular culture. What is more realistic is to learn which gestures that are acceptable in your culture are unacceptable in another. For example, the "okay" sign means "fine" in American and German cultures, but in Portugal, Brazil, Spain, Russia, Paraguay, and Uruguay, it is considered an obscene gesture. In Japan, the "okay" sign means "money."

In Australia, the "thumbs up" sign, which in the United States, Great Britain, or Russia means "great" or "terrific," can be considered rude in Australia and offensive in Iran.

The "thumbs down" sign is rude in Greece; it indicates condemnation in Canada and the United States.

Appropriate body language, how to stand or sit (for example, in the Middle East it is considered impolite to show the sole of your shoes if you cross your legs), as well as facial expressions, the use of silence, and how much personal space is considered appropriate, will all vary from culture to culture. Some cultures have so little space between individuals that someone could be tempted to back away. But doing so could be considered rude, potentially sabotaging the new or developing business relationship.

---

**CONSIDERATION #11**
**NEGOTIATING STYLES**

---

This topic is so pivotal to doing business globally that it is the subject of Chapter 8, "Negotiating." For now, let's consider what Tufts University law professor Jeswald Salacuse, author of two highly-regarded books on global negotiating, *Making Global Deals,* and *The Global Negotiator*, has to say on the subject. Salacuse lists ten simple negotiating rules in *Making Global Deals*. Here are three:

- *Prepare thoroughly.* In addition to knowing everything about the transaction, become an expert in the cultures and countries involved in the deal.

- *Form relationships.* Move your socializing away from the negotiating table. Display a sincere concern for the other party's country and culture.

- *Keep your cool.* How much emotion a culture will tolerate in negotiations varies widely. In the United States, it might be acceptable to make an angry comment when negotiating, whereas in Thailand, that same comment might be considered proof of insanity.

---

**CONSIDERATION #12**
**TOPICS OR POLITICALLY INCORRECT ISSUES TO AVOID**

---

Although most of this is common sense, it is still a good idea to check with someone you trust in a particular country, or at least do some reading on the country so you have a very clear list of topics to avoid. For example, don't talk about poverty in India or communism in Russia.

A 42-year-old sales executive in Germany added that in doing business with Germans, he suggests "avoiding digging too deep into current politics. Most people you meet in business tend to be conservative but some aren't and it would be an awkward situation either way." Also, German history is difficult, whether it is the Third Reich or the '89 reunification. Everyone will probably answer as expected (anti-Nazi and pro-unification) but would consider this an embarrassing examination of their sentiments."

## CONSIDERATION #13
## GIFT GIVING AND RECEIVING

When is it expected that you will bring a gift to a business associate? Usually if you visit someone in their home a gift is expected but in some countries, like China, according to recent business travelers with whom I spoke it is customary to bring a gift, especially a food gift, to those with whom you are having a business meeting. However, as pointed out in *Kiss, Bow or Shake Hands*, "gift giving is a sensitive issue in China. Technically, it is against the law, but the acceptance of gift giving is increasing." The website 1worldglobalgifts.com advises, "If you wish to give a gift to an individual, you must do it privately, in the context of friendship, not business."

What about gift giving if you exhibit at, or attend, a trade show? When I attend the Frankfurt Book Fair, there are several agents or publishers that I meet with from various cultures, especially Germany and Taiwan, who like to offer a token gift of chocolate or a writing-related gift, like a pen or note cards, at the beginning of the business meeting. It would be considered impolite to reject the gift or to avoid making a fuss over it. I will discuss these issues in greater detail later on in the book, in Chapter 7, "Gift-Giving, Legal Considerations, and Ethics," but in general, consider how much money you should spend on a gift so as not to offend your host or be accused of being too extravagant. Avoid spending too much so that that you might be considered giving or taking a bribe, but avoid spending so little, or buying something so flimsy that you would be perceived as being cheap or having poor taste.

| CONSIDERATION #14 |
| HOLIDAYS AND VACATION TIME |

When first doing business internationally, whether by e-mail or in preparing for an international business trip, it is important to consider the time of year in the other country as well as whether or not it will be a holiday or vacation time. For example, there is a week in early winter when many Asian countries, including China, Indonesia, Vietnam, Korea, and Taiwan celebrate what is called the Lunar Celebration or New Year. Companies shut down for an entire week. Even before the week-long celebration begins, work is winding down in preparation for that holiday. Trying to push through new business or negotiations with practically everyone focused on their upcoming holiday plans would be like setting up a business meeting in Manhattan late on the Friday before Memorial Day weekend.

Vacation time varies widely around the world with American businessmen or businesswomen having just one or two weeks, while school teachers, students, or those who are self-employed may take more time. In other countries, especially France, Germany, Spain, and the five countries of Scandinavia- Norway, Denmark, Sweden, Finland, and Iceland—taking July and August or at least the entire month of August as a vacation from work is typical and expected.

Failing to plan business trips according to those local customs can lead to frustration and hard feelings. For example, it may be more convenient for you to travel to Spain or Italy during August, but it will be hard for you to find anyone there who is willing to meet with you since that is their vacation time and it's likely that they will be out of town.

In most Muslim countries, Fridays are not work days; some workers also do not work on Thursdays, but do work on Sundays. In Israel, business typically is not conducted during the Jewish Sabbath, which is from sundown on Friday night till sundown on Saturday, as well as during the holidays of Yom Kippur and Passover.

Many European enterprises close early on Friday afternoon during the summer to allow employees to escape early for the weekend from Memorial Day (the end of May) until Labor Day (the beginning of September). This pattern is typical for a number of American businesses as well, especially in those states where the pleasant weather is only available during the shortened summertime. As noted, some European businesses close down for the entire month of August or at least for three weeks, to allow everyone to take a vacation from work, which is believed to lead to greater operational efficiency and cost-savings as well as to the work-life balance that so many in the United States (typified internationally by what is still called the "Protestant work ethic," which means working long hours with little leisure time) are trying to achieve.

Chinese New Year, also called Lunar New Year or Spring Festival, which usually occurs sometime between the third week of January and the middle of February with the exact dates changing form year to year. Businesses close down for a week during the Lunar New year in countries where a major part of the population celebrates this traditional Chinese holiday dating back centuries including Mainland China, Vietnam, Indonesia, Malaysia, Singapore, Taiwan, Indonesia.

Finally, different countries have their own celebrations for independence days and religious festivals. On these days most banks, businesses and government offices in those countries are closed. The British, Canadians and Europeans in general celebrate their "Labor Day" on May 1, and not on the first Monday in September as in the U.S. The British and Canadians, however, do throw in a "bank holiday" at the end of August to give people an extra three-day holiday to mark the end of the summer vacation season.

*International holidays are listed, among other places at https://www.bank-holidays.com, and www.infoplease.com/ipa. The U.S. Department of Commerce's website www.Export.gov also provides complete information on the business week and business days and holidays in countries around the world.*

International holidays are listed, among other places at https://www.bank-holidays.com, and www.infoplease.com/ipa. The U.S. Department of Commerce's website www.Export.gov also provides complete information on the business week and business days and holidays in countries around the world.

## CONSIDERATION #15
## RELIGIOUS PRACTICES AND RELATED CONCERNS

It is not necessary to have a detailed knowledge of every religion in the world, but it would be helpful to know what religions are common in what regions and what the basic tenets of those religions are. In addition, you also want to be careful not to mock any set of beliefs, whether or not you agree with any or all of its principles. There are dozens of religions throughout the world but the key faiths are: Buddhism; Judaism; Christianity (including Catholicism and Protestantism); Confucianism; Hinduism; Islam; Jainism; Shinto; Sikhism; and Taoism. There also are those who define themselves as agnostic (believing in God but not a particular set of beliefs) and atheists (those who do not believe in God at all).

When you are visiting another country, your business colleague/host may take you sightseeing including a visit to a sacred shrine. Do not be surprised if you are expected to remove your shoes as is their custom.

In general, most Hindus are vegetarians. It is not necessary for you to be a vegetarian but if you are visiting India and sharing a business lunch with vegetarians, you might want to avoid eating meat because it could offend them. You might similarly avoid ordering pork if you are having a business dinner with someone who is Jewish, especially if that individual is orthodox and kosher.

In the United States, it generally is best to avoid a discussion about religion in business-related situations. That basic business protocol applies internationally as well. An individual's religious beliefs are very sacred and personal; showing respect for someone else's religion, including having at least a working knowledge of its history and beliefs, is not the same thing as agreeing with that religion.

Keep in mind that if you plan to conduct business internationally you will need to master the key fifteen international protocol concerns that were highlighted in this chapter, whether you are going to Korea for a meeting with the head of sales at a company, or you are hosting a dinner at a restaurant near your Chicago office for the president of a company based in Mumbai, India who just happens to be a vegetarian.

# CHAPTER 3

# Build Global Relationships First
# And the Business Will Follow

In America, for some, relationships tend to develop *out of* doing business, but in other parts of the world, Asia in particular, there has to be a relationship first before any business is even conducted. As the relationship strengthens and grows, so does the business. (There is, however, a growing trend in the United States toward relationship first, then business, due to increased fears of unwittingly hiring someone with a questionable reputation, or who might not take the company in the right direction.)

Building relationships internationally can be challenging for those Americans who sometimes lack the patience required to invest in connections without the guarantee of someday doing business together.

When it comes to building business relationships in other countries, it is important to understand that there are generally two distinctive relationship "types": one that is strictly business; and the other that involves a friendship.

In some cultures, such as Indonesia, it is said that you need to first establish the friendship and then business will follow. In other countries, it is the norm to keep friendship and business separate to the point that doing business together may actually rule out becoming friends, at least as long as the business relationship persists. Yet, if friendship and business are kept separate, in many cultures there is still a preference for long-term relationships, even if it remains more business than personal.

In Italy, it is important that any business relationship begins through a personal contact. That means you have to connect with someone locally who already has a business relationship with the person or company that you are trying to approach.

The bigger the business deal, the more important the personal connection. The ideal way to build an international business relationship is to begin with a face-to-face meeting, despite the distances. In Japan they call it a "courtesy call."

Law professor Jeswald W. Salacuse, an expert in global negotiations, found himself making several such "courtesy calls" to land a major corporate grant. He made four trans-Pacific visits to Japan and initiated a number of calls. What he found was that his willingness to make those courtesy calls or visits showed the executive at the corporation that he was seriously interested and sincere. It also provided opportunities for the executive to get to know Professor Salacuse and for a relationship to develop.

> The bigger the business deal, the more important the personal connection. The ideal way to build an international business relationship is to begin with a face-to-face meeting, despite the distances. In Japan they call it a "courtesy call."

Japanese business expert Rochelle Kopp of Japan Intercultural Consulting defines the courtesy call as stopping by "without a specific agenda." Conversely, in the United States, we're often so busy that too often we consider something like that a waste of time. (Even over the phone, if you call someone in business in the U.S. just to say hello, he or she may even pose the question to you, "What can I do for you?" or, even more bluntly, "And why are you calling?") Kopp says that in Japan it is common to just stop by and have a cup of tea and talk about anything *but* business. As Kopp puts it, "Japanese love to chit-chat so be prepared to talk quite a bit. You want to find out about the people you're working with. What part of Japan are they from? What are their hobbies? They'll ask you similar questions about hobbies and sports, that sort of thing."

It is all a prelude leading up to a meeting that will *eventually* involve a conversation about business. Kopp adds that in Japan, every time you are going to meet with people, you bring them something. Usually it's something to eat or candy. Whenever Kopp travels to Japan for business, she takes two suitcases—one for her clothes and a larger one filled with the candy that she will give out as gifts.

Even if a particular culture has a "rule" about keeping business and friendship or personal relationships separate, if two individuals care about each other and there is a spark of friendship between them, it will develop naturally on its own. However, it can be useful to know which countries discourage personal relationships in business. That way, if someone does not encourage developing a personal relationship within a business setting, you are less likely to take it personally.

But cultural differences in how to approach relationships in business should be seen as only guidelines. In reality, each relationship will develop on its own merits.

A film director and producer from Venezuela, for example, says that that in her culture, if she has a friendship with someone in business and something comes up that would force her to choose between the business and the friendship, she would put the friendship first.

## THE BEGINNING OF A GLOBAL RELATIONSHIP

The first step in building any international relationship is the initial contact.

Consider if you are at a higher or lower level with the person with whom you are trying to connect. Will the disparity in levels be a hindrance to doing business together, as well as to developing an immediate or long-term relationship? Taking the time to figure out if you should be connecting to a specific person in the first place can help alleviate some conflicts down the road. My research has found that befriending at the same level is the least risky and safest type of business connection.

> *Taking the time to figure out if you should be connecting to a specific person in the first place can help alleviate some conflicts down the road.*

Connecting for business does not always have to mean that you need to go over to another country and meet with those with whom you plan to do business first-hand. The system that I was taught when I had my first job in foreign rights at Grove Press, Inc. was that I connected to local agents, and that they would have the relationships with the buyers in their various countries. Although it is certainly a plus to go to the local agent's country for a face-to-face meeting, you can also meet at trade shows held around the world and then follow-up by phone or e-mail. In that way, you are putting your energy into the relationship you have with the local agents who live in the countries where you want to do business. They will be forging the relationships with the local buyers; they will give you the entre to new business. Those local agents will also help you to avoid saying or doing something embarrassing; they can suggest how to present a project or a concept so it is more likely to be accepted by businesses or, if selling a product internationally, by the people of their culture and country.

John A. Caslione and Andrew R. Thomas have some wonderful examples in their book, *Global Manifest Destiny*, of companies that needed local agents or affiliates to avoid many a language *faux pas*. Here are some of the examples they share, which of course, were ultimately changed from the literal translations noted below so the language would be appropriate and culturally viable:

- General Motors' Body by Fisher in Flemish became "Corps by Fisher."

- Pepsi-Cola's slogan "Come alive with Pepsi" in the Chinese version of *Reader's Digest* instead became "'Pepsi brings your ancestors back from the grave."

- Frank Perdue's slogan "It takes a tough man to make a tender chicken" instead became in Spanish "It takes a virile man to make chicken affectionate."

The publishing world often uses agents, known as foreign or co-agents when the agent is based in another country, to help oversee the translation of a book title and sometimes even the book itself, making sure especially in the title that the author's original intent is not lost in translation as in the above corporate examples.

Other businesses often use a similar approach to enlisting the help of locals so someone new to the culture can be on a fast learning curve. Barry Petersen, senior correspondent for CBS News, has spent the last twenty-five years working and living in countries around the world, mostly Japan, China, and Moscow. Petersen has found the best way for him to quickly learn what he needs to know about a new culture is to find what he calls the "pathfinder" to help him assimilate into the new culture. Petersen says he didn't have time to do much preparation when he moved to Japan but when he got there, he read everything he could.

"I read books like the one you're writing," Peterson told me. "I talked to people who lived there or had lived there. I did some research. Reading is critical. My research had to happen simultaneously with living in the place. I did the same thing with moving to Moscow. I think this is really a key point: if you are going to a place like this, if you are going to do business, find the pathfinders who have gone ahead of you. They know where the pot holes are. They know where the signs are, where you should turn right when you think you should turn left."

Speaker and entrepreneur Dr. Gayle Carson has had successful speaking engagements in venues around the world. Finding a local sponsor is pivotal for her whenever she travels and works internationally. For Dr. Carson, a "sponsor" is similar to Petersen's "pathfinder" or to local foreign agents for publishers or other agents doing business in other countries. This way Carson knows she will be compensated for her work, stay in the best hotels, and not have a transportation problem while there. (Of course, the sponsor must be checked out and have a positive history.)

Dr. Carson also points out the additional business benefits of having a local sponsor: she developed a business relationship with a sponsor she used in Indonesia for five years and he also brought her additional bookings, which she shared with him. When people became familiar with her books, which were in the bookstores when she was there, they began to get in touch with her for presentations. So she put them in touch with her local sponsor to do all the negotiations.

How do you find a sponsor? According to Dr. Carson, it isn't easy but it is worth taking the time to find one. Carson said her sponsor in Indonesia heard her speak at a conference he attended. Today, however, it's much easier because of the Internet since you can post information or even videos that share your background or show your presentation skills. There are other ways to find a sponsor depending on the industry that you are working in. For speakers, check out training companies in the country you wish to visit. Dr. Carson's sponsor was with a well-established training company in Jakarta who had a lot of connections with banks and oil companies.

You could also contact companies that specialize in finding local opportunities for your particular skill set, such as speaker bureaus for speakers; for all kinds of skills and businesses, check out the American offices of large companies in that country, or the American Chambers of Commerce. All the member companies who could possibly use you are potential sources of global opportunities.

Says Dr. Carson: "It is much easier for an American to work with an American counterpart of a company in another country. There are also consulting firms who can use your services. If you only contact these people, they will refer you on to other people who can help you."

Dr. Carson's advice can be applied to a broad array of service providers looking to work internationally; every skill-set from teaching to translating, coaching to editing may find her strategy useful.

## Connecting through Networking Websites[1]

Today, two of the fastest ways to initiate an international business relationship are through online networking websites such as LinkedIn.com or xing.com. There is a misconception that LinkedIn.com is mainly a U.S./domestic phenomenon. It is actually very global with businessmen and businesswomen signing up for the free LinkedIn.com as far back as 2004. There is also xing.com for business networking with members throughout Europe and India.

You will probably have a core group of relationships at LinkedIn.com made up of people who really know you, like you, and admire you and your services or products. This should include those who have worked with you who will recommend you. These are the people on whom you can depend to sing your praises.

Start with those you know and ask them to introduce you to others internationally with whom you could connect. Start with your first tier of

---

[1] See Strategy #56 "Use Social Networking to Improve Your Work Relationships," in my book, *Productive Relationships: 57 Strategies for Building Stronger Business Connections* (Hannacroix Creek Books, Inc., 2011) for a more in-depth discussion of using Linkedin.com, Twitter.com, and Facebook.com.

relationships and also begin with those who are less likely to see you as a competitor so that they will more likely give you referrals.

The recommendation letters that you get on LinkedIn are as important as the way you write your profile. Therefore, ask the person writing the recommendation if you can review his or her recommendation, just for accuracy and nuance, before sending it in. LinkedIn will give you the opportunity to review a recommendation letter so you can decide if you want to accept it and have it posted or not. But it will be harder to ask the person who recommended you to rewrite the reference at that point than if you made sure that you were pleased with the recommendation letter in the first place.

Also remember that everything you write on LinkedIn is basically public, not just to your connections but to the entire world since your profile may be posted on the Internet and available for everyone to read unless you have asked to keep your profile restricted to just LinkedIn.com. Especially if your profile is public, make sure everything is okay (e.g., if you have a job and are looking for a new job, be careful about announcing that since your current boss and coworkers could see it in your bio or status update); so post with caution.

But be careful not to tout your products to your potential or ongoing international buyers or contacts via Linkedin.com or you could get a bad reputation for being too self-serving, self-promotional, and/or too heavy-handed in the selling department. You get by giving on Linkedin.com and xing.com. Provide links to informative articles that your colleagues might find useful. Share about upcoming events such as in-person lectures, conferences, or webinars that might be of interest. With international social networking sites, being subtle works better than being too pushy about your business goals.

You want to build up relationships and, if possible, take it from online to in-person by attending networking events like the one I was invited to in Austria that was attended by approximately 150 xing.com members.

There are other ways to find people. Go to their websites, find their e-mail addresses and communicate directly. You could also make a phone call, even if you have to call another country, and introduce yourself. Let that person know if you have any colleagues in common or, even if you do not and this was a cold call, explain why he or she might want to start a business relationship with you.

Remember that it is rare to find someone today who is not busy and pressed for time and who is looking to connect just to grow their network. Linkedin.com is *not* a matchmaking service for business people. It is a tool for growing your business, so make sure you have a clear business reason for wanting to seek someone out.

Be prepared that it will take time to grow your business relationships internationally. This can be challenging for some Americans who are used to a "go, go, go" approach to business. They may feel it just isn't their style to take the months or even years to develop trust and mutual respect in order to do one or multiple deals in countries such as Japan and India. But if you put the time and effort into growing your business relationships, these connections can last far longer than in the United States where, so often, getting the best price or deal has replaced continuity in business based on loyalty.

You also have to be prepared that if you are developing an international business relationship, you may find yourself invited to your colleague's family event, such as a wedding or anniversary party; you will be expected to attend, just as you would back home. Only back home it might be a question of traveling across town or purchasing a gift. But with international business relationships, it could mean traveling half-way around the world at considerable cost. These types of invitations can put your commitment to the international relationships to the "test." If you fail, all the time you have invested in developing this relationship, and the business that went with it, may be jeopardized. If you are unable to attend a major life event of your international friend, if appropriate, send a gift and card and make sure your friend knows your intentions far enough in advance so you will not be expected.

In some countries, such as Hungary, France, or Italy, you may want to have a local representative, distributor, or middle man to introduce you in business. If so, choose this person carefully because your foreign partners may demand a contract for a minimum of a year or longer that requires exclusivity. Unless either party asks to cancel the contract, it typically will be automatically renewed on an annual basis after that time.

## GROWING YOUR INTERNATIONAL RELATIONSHIPS

Because relationships are so pivotal in doing business internationally, make the time and financial commitment to do whatever it takes to keep your various foreign connections strong and current. Call, e-mail, or visit and bring your foreign business partners up to date about yourself and your products or services. Send out a regular electronic or print newsletter or letter about what is happening with your business but try to make it as personalized as possible, such as handwriting a short note along with whatever is being shared in a general way if you are sending a print version.

Do not just rely on social media sites alone to keep up your relationships whether on Facebook, Linkedin.com, MySpace, Plaxo, xing.com, or others. Set aside money from your budget to travel to meet with your foreign partners, clients, or customers, keeping in mind what month or time of year will be most convenient for them. Try to avoid the summer months because of vacations in Europe or the winter Christmas break if you are visiting South America, Australia or New Zealand, which is their summer vacation as well as their time to take a break because of the holidays.

Do not take it personally if you want to go to Paris in August and your local business connection will not find time to even have a cup of coffee with you. If you are business associates, and not friends, no business is conducted during the August vacation month. If the relationship is that important to you, visit at another time, when it is appropriate and convenient for your French colleague or customer, such as October, March, or May.

In my book, *Productive Relationships: 57 Strategies for Building Stronger Business Connections*, almost all of those 57 strategies can be applied to enhancing your international, not just your local, business relationships. (See especially the 21 strategies detailed in Chapters 5 through 7 including Chapter 5, "Getting Along Better," Chapter 6, "Coping with a Range of Workplace Situations," and Chapter 7, "Improve Workplace or Business Relationships" which includes Strategy #44, "Tackle Cultural and International Issues."

You may find the advice in Strategy #25, "Be a Principled Person," useful in growing your international relationships; it is adapted and reprinted here, with permission:

1. Have mutual respect. You're not the only one trying to make things work at the office (or in this international business relationship), even though it's human nature to be more focused on your own career and your own advancement than anyone else's.
2. Share a commitment to getting along with each and everyone you work with or that you report to, locally or internationally.
3. Understand the personal or cultural boundaries to the relationship as defined by each participant in the relationship and keep those boundaries in mind.
4. Keep all confidences, work-related and personal.
5. Deal with conflicts or disagreements immediately and appropriately.
6. Avoid holding a grudge even if you were right and you were wronged.
7. Make sure someone earns your trust before you share something that could be used against you or shared indiscriminately even if done by accident or in jest.
8. Before you get offended or angry, listen to the other person's explanation or perspective. There may be facts, extenuating circumstances, or cultural differences you do not know about that help explain a situation that you misconstrued.
9. Emphasize your similarities and shared goals, interests, values, or beliefs rather than creating a wedge by dwelling on your differences.
10. Share credit, as appropriate, so you get labeled a "we" not just a "me" colleague or business associate.

## CONFLICTS AND ENDINGS

There are many cultures where saying "no" involves a loss of face and therefore "no" is to be avoided at all costs. That is why it is so crucial to meet with those you want to do business with internationally as often as possible, whether at a trade show, in their office, in your office, or even having a videoconference whereby you can see your associate's body language. The body language can be quite telling; it may convey what someone is really thinking about a potential deal or offer, despite what they might be saying.

Most cultures prefer to avoid direct confrontation so you need to stay calm and try to figure out what is causing a conflict rather than getting upset or making accusations about being ignored or needing an answer right away. In many cultures, silence is the most polite way to indicate that there is no interest in a product or deal that has been offered. Since in some countries there is also an emphasis on loyalty to a particular company, distributor, or retailer, before you throw in the towel with this business relationship, if possible, offer a different product. He or she might find that of interest and you will be surprised to see how quickly the communication between the two of you is back on track again.

It is preferable to avoid writing negative things in e-mails to your international business relationship as a way to work out your differences. Since the misunderstandings might be cultural, if you cannot discuss your conflicts in person, at least try to have a phone conversation that will enable you to figure out what is causing the misunderstanding. Is there an expectation that is not being met? Was a promise made for delivery of goods or payment for an agreed upon project that has not been received? If you usually meet at a trade show and your friend neglected to keep time open in his schedule, are you feeling discounted?

The British cliché of the "stiff upper lip" will serve you well in keeping the peace with your international business relationships. Unless you are truly the best of friends and you feel absolutely comfortable sharing your "feelings," it might be better to avoid confrontations that are more emotional than business-oriented, especially if your job or business is at stake.

Ending a business arrangement should be done with grace and style so you do not risk getting a bad reputation in that industry or region. Fortunately, if you and your foreign business associate signed a formal contract, there will probably be a clause right in the contract about how to handle a termination. You could look to the contract for guidance, pointing out that you are invoking a specific clause in your contract and you thank them for doing business with you. You are sorry it did not work out in the long run.

If your business was based on a shared agreement and a handshake, or informal e-mails back and forth, be firm but pleasant about the necessity of immediately terminating your relationship and again express your sincere regrets that the relationship did not work out for the long term.

Be as cordial and as pleasant as possible even in another country since you do not want to be badmouthed. With the way that companies are buying up other companies, the individual or company you dismiss today may turn out to be the buyer of another company that you choose to do business with tomorrow.

Emphasize that you like someone personally and that ending the business is no reflection on them but it is a purely business decision. You may be ending the business relationship because you and a particular individual just don't hit it off, but you don't want to say that or put it in writing. No one likes to be personally rejected—whatever their culture. Incurring the wrath of someone you are terminating can be much more devastating than blaming it on a business reason. That is why it is so important to be attentive to those with whom you are doing business. If there is a strong, personal connection, you or your international partner might overlook the less-positive business aspects because the personal relationship aspect is so strong.

# CHAPTER 4

# Rules of the Road:
## Country by Country Etiquette

The information in this chapter is based on my experiences doing business with each of the countries that are discussed. This includes those countries I have personally visited or completed deals with over the Internet, phone, or through meeting at an international trade show. In addition to my own first-hand experiences, I also conducted numerous interviews with people who either live and work in these countries, or have traveled to these countries on business.

There are entire books written on doing business with each of the countries that follow, as well as courses offered by numerous associations, government, or private companies (some suggestions are included in the Resource section in the back of this book). My goal in this chapter is to provide a very basic overview for doing business with someone from each country, whether in-person or virtually.

### Australia

Three years ago, when I was in Sydney, Melbourne, and Brisbane for business, one of the challenges I faced was making sure I understood everyone, even though we were all speaking English. At times, I found someone's accent made it hard to decipher every word; I had to listen very carefully especially if someone spoke too quickly.

I did commit one *faux pas* when I cancelled an invitation to a colleague's home for a barbecue. I had already accepted her invitation to me and my family, who had accompanied me on my business trip, but we had just spent the day fighting rush hour traffic outside of Sydney to go to another dinner and wanted to take a day off from having to travel again. I later learned that being invited to someone's home for a barbecue is a very big deal in Australia. To turn down such an invitation, or to cancel one after you have accepted, except for the most dramatic of reasons, is not very polite. My colleague has since forgiven me but I know now that I will never do it again.

Each of the three cities I traveled to in Australia had a very distinctive flavor and style, You should be careful not to talk about "Australia" based on visiting just one city or area any more than you would travel to the United States and act as if Manhattan represented the entire country, or that Chicago is the same as New Orleans or Los Angeles. Australia is a vast and diverse country with a lot of land but the population is dramatically smaller compared to its size, 21 million people (compared to over 300 million in the United States or 142 million people in Russia). The bulk of Australia's population is focused on the east coast with its best-known cities of Sydney and Melbourne. The western part of the country is sparsely populated.

Talking about the origins of Australia is like talking about the way that the early settlers in America "stole" the land from the Indians. You should not discuss the fact that New South Wales was a penal colony from 1788 to 1823 with convicts from Britain, or bring up the controversial topic of the Aborigine people who are among the oldest cultures in the world.

I discovered that Australians resent being lumped together with New Zealanders. The countries are closer to each other than they are to other countries since both are islands and can be as near as a two-hour plane ride. Residents of both speak English, but they are distinct countries with unique histories and contemporary cultures and peoples.

Australians were very concerned that I chose to visit when it was their winter, which is the summertime in the United States, even though their winter was, by and large, rather mild, in the 50s or 60s, compared to the frigid cold I was used to in the eastern United States.

Karen Robertson, who runs a small publishing company and who moved to Sydney, Australia with her husband Chris from the United States, says you should avoid using "Aussie" slang like "sheila," "bloke," or "mate." Just speak as you always would. A lot of the shows on Australian TV are

American so Australians are used to the way Americans talk and are familiar with American customs.

If you go out with those you meet at work or through business, Robertson suggests that it's useful to know some of the drinking customs. Australians enjoy dining out and many like to have a drink. It's very common to go to a pub or bar after work when entertaining, instead of going directly to a restaurant. One thing that it might take time to get comfortable with at the bar is "the shout." Basically, if you go to a bar or pub, someone might say "it's my shout" and they'll buy a round of drinks for everyone. Then, another person will offer to shout and do the same. (It's bad form to order an expensive drink on someone's else's shout, like a cocktail, and then buy yourself something cheap on your own shout.)

Chris Robertson adds: "If it's advice for an American doing business in Australia, I'd be heading straight to the issue that Australians are more informal than Americans in a business context. Typically don't get straight to business when meeting. A bit of pleasantries and getting to know each other is typical. It's worth a warning: the first impressions Australians have of American is that they're loud and over confident. Australians are sharp and aware. Don't fall into the trap of thinking you're in a backwater community."

As noted before, being aggressive or too "hard sell" are traits that backfire in doing business in or with Australia. Australians don't respond well to aggression. As with America, good manners are always good form. It is also important to Australians that you take time to build a relationship with them as part of doing business together.

## BRAZIL

If you go to Brazil for business, expect just a handshake at the start of your meeting. But don't be offended if at the end of the meeting, the other person touches your arm or your shoulder. It's just a gesture of friendship. Women who have a strong positive feeling toward each other in business may also kiss each other European style, on two cheeks, at the beginning and end of their meeting.

The biggest *faux pas* you can make in Brazil is to assume that they speak Spanish. Portuguese is the official language and Spanish is not spoken at all. You will find many people who speak English in Brazil, especially in business, but the taxi drivers don't and as you leave the major cities and go into the more rural areas, the average citizens will probably not know English, either. Be prepared to bring along a business team associate who speaks Portuguese, or to hire a translator to help you in your meetings.

Brazil is considered part of BRIC—Brazil, Russian, India, and China—four countries that are said to be fast-growing economic forces and attractive for business consideration.

Brazil is the fifth largest country in the world, and heavily populated with 192 million citizens, yet few Americans know much about it. An anomaly among its Spanish-speaking neighbors, Brazil's affinity is to Portugal, which colonized the country in 1500. It gained its independence 300 years later in 1822. Ironically, its European counterpart has a relatively small population of just 11 million people. The Portuguese spoken in Portugal is slightly different from the Portuguese spoken in Brazil. (If you are selling foreign rights to a book for translation into Portuguese, it is considered two separate sales, one to Brazil and another to Portugal.)

Anyone doing business today and in the next decade going forward would do well to find out more about the business opportunities in Brazil as well as its customs and culture. With the hosting of the World Cup in 2014 and the Olympics in Rio de Janeiro in 2016, awareness of Brazil is bound to increase.

## CANADA

Canada is another vast country but it has a relatively small population for its size: 33 million people. It may be useful to know the population of Canada so you can avoid the common mistake of assuming it is as populated as it is vast. Another annoyance to Canadians is being considered an extension of the United States because it shares a border as well as a language. Knowing that French is the second official language in Canada is important as well as the regions in Canada where French is spoken: Quebec, and in some parts of Nova Scotia and New Brunswick.

Some Canadians are offended if those doing business with them are ignorant about who their political leaders are, since they will know so much about the United States and who its leaders are.

In business, Canadians tend to be more formal and conservative than Americans in how they dress and interact.

Ray Bowman, of Bowman Business Services, has done extensive business with Canadians. He urges any American who plans on doing business with Canada to learn as much as possible about the country. He's amazed that he still finds people who aren't sure whether Canada is a real country. He says Americans are very bad at showing respect for Canada even though Canada is its biggest trading partner.

In Canada, business entertaining is more likely to occur in a restaurant or a nightclub than in someone's home. And, while you might send a gift after a business deal has closed, gifts are generally not presented upon meeting someone or at the beginning of negotiations.

There is universal healthcare in Canada, a system they are very proud of, that offers free access to medical facilities, such as hospitals, and to physician services, based on need rather than ability to pay. It is a *faux pas*, however, to call their system of healthcare "socialism" or to intimate that it is the same system offered in the United Kingdom. Interestingly, Canada is among the top ten major countries in the world for life expectancy.

## CHINA

Martin vanDerSchouw is CEO and president of Looking Glass Development, a performance management company that he founded in 1999. vanDerShouw, who divides his time between Victoria, British Columbia and Denver, Colorado, when he is not traveling internationally, has made numerous trips to China. He shares what he has learned about international business protocol issues from his business dealings in China:

"It's very different from the mindset that the American businessman is used to. There are two aspects that you need to deal with there. First, there is a government aspect that comes into play with everything in China because it is a totalitarian state. You need to develop strong relations with government officials and the appropriate government official for whatever you want to do. That is absolutely critical.

"The second thing is to understand how decisions are made in China. If you're in a meeting and you're presenting information and their heads are nodding, Americans take that to mean agreement. But to an Asian, that typically means 'I hear you.' What's happening in those scenarios is that they want to talk about it amongst themselves. Americans will think they had a deal but the Chinese will come back and say that they want to do the exact opposite."

Another aspect of doing business in China is to be aware of how important your IP (intellectual property) is to you. I've known people who have gotten incredibly frustrated with copyright violation. You have to think about it ahead of time. How are you going to protect your rights and what is yours?

As in most countries around the world with complicated and especially divergent business practices, Martin recommends having a local agent or representative who is an extension of your business. Says Martin: "One of the strategies that is most helpful is to literally get someone who comes highly recommended who is Chinese who will represent you over there. Someone who lives there not someone who has traveled to China or just lived there for a couple of months."

Martin notes that one of the biggest *faux pas* to avoid in China is criticism of the government or of anything that is going on.

Also be aware that in China, you are not supposed to finish your food. That indicates that you haven't been taken care of and that you need more. In America, we are taught to clean our plates.

Finally, when Martin travels to China he leaves it up to his local representative or agent to buy an appropriate gift. "It was usually something relevant to what we were doing like an autographed copy of a book or something specific to where we were from. The one thing to avoid is trinkets that are obviously $5 and not of any value."

## FRANCE

The French are very proud of their official language, French. If you are visiting France for business, and you do not know French, you should apologize for your situation. You can also show politeness by at least starting your meeting with *Bon jour*, and ending it, when you are saying goodbye, with *Au revoir*.

Handshakes are typical when you meet for the first time in business but as a relationship develops, women in business will kiss each other on the cheek, first one cheek and then the other. The French are very expressive people and they may speak with their hands and stand closer to you than you are used to.

The French take their summer vacations and holidays very seriously so avoid trying to schedule a business meeting when it is a holiday or vacation time if you want to stay on your business colleague's good side. Loyalty is very important to the French; they expect to do business with the same people for many years and if they doubt that you share that perspective, they may expect to lock you into it through an exclusive contract.

Discussing business over a meal or at a café is very typical in France but you might also meet in the office for business if you do not have a personal relationship.

In addition to their language, the French take their lunchtime very seriously. It can last as long as two hours and it is the ideal time to grow your business relationship. Because lunch is such a big part of the workday, if you are not going to lunch for business, the ideal times for business meetings in someone's office would be before 11 a.m. and after 3:30 p.m.

## GERMANY

With 82 million people strong, and its capital of Berlin, a vibrant city, Germany is an economic leader in Western Europe. Its business orientation is a formal one with a handshake the expected way to greet in business and a business suit and tie the typical dress in most situations. Only in certain industries, like film or fine arts, is more casual dress permissible.

When meeting someone for the first time, present your business card and do not expect a lot of small talk before you get right to the heart of your reason for meeting. Avoid asking personal questions especially when you meet for the first time. In Germany, they tend to keep their personal and business lives separate until you have formed a strong personal bond.

German is the official language but most businesspeople speak English. Taxi cab drivers, even in major cities like Frankfurt, may not know enough English to discuss where you are going so make sure you have your destination written down clearly so they can plug it into their GPS system, if they have one, or ask someone else for help.

In keeping with the separation of personal and business relationships, business entertaining is rarely done in one's private apartment or home. It is a tribute to you if you are invited to someone's private home for a meal; do not turn that offer down for that would be extremely offensive to your host or hostess. Germans are very proud of their beers and wines. If you do not drink alcohol, do not make a big deal about it since this could offend someone.

Avoid giving a gift if it might be misinterpreted as an attempt to influence the outcome of a negotiation. Your German counterpart might give you chocolates or a token gift of food representative of their country.

The wall separating East and West Germany came down in 1990; since that time, Germany has been a united country although it is still taking time for the previously-communist-run East to catch up with the more prosperous West.

In time, you may be able to build up a personal as well as a professional relationship with those you do business with in Germany, but trying to hurry the process along could backfire. Since business is between companies and not just between individuals it can be easier to shift who you deal with at a company from one person to another. This situation could arise if someone leaves the firm or you think you need to find someone with whom you have a better rapport, or who has more authority, than the person with whom you are dealing.

Avoid getting too emotional in your interactions or negotiations. In terms of negotiating style and contracts, haggling is not part of the German approach so try to start off with a firm idea of what you will or will not accept and do not expect the price of an offer to move higher than 25% from the initial one until the final agreement is signed.

Avoid talking about World War II, anti-Semitism, the holocaust, Adolf Hitler, the Wall, or Israel.

Punctuality is expected in Germany and you should definitely be on time for meetings. You should also promptly follow-up with whatever promises you have made during any meetings.

Since Germans prefer to be non-confrontational, try to meet in person as much as possible. You could learn more about their true intentions around a proposed deal or business venture from their body language or silences as much from their words. Don't automatically assume that silence following an interruption automatically equals a negative decision. It might reflect that someone is totally overwhelmed with business or personal matters. Do not take that silence personally unless you have additional corroboration through a phone call or any in-person meetings that you manage to arrange down the road. That is why it may be useful to have a local representative who is helping you with your business efforts in Germany. Unless you travel frequently to Germany, they will have a better chance of figuring out what is really going on with the various business opportunities you are currently involved in or that you are exploring.

## INDIA

India's 1.2 billion people are a religiously diverse population with 120 million Muslims. Do not make the assumption that the person you are meeting with is Hindu although 83% practice that religion. The rest of the population is divided among Christians, Sikhs, Jains, Buddhists, and Parsis with their own distinct cultures.

Although English is the predominant language, there are a dozen other languages that are also spoken in different parts of the country. English will take you quite far in the business community. But if you are trying to impress someone, you might consider learning a few words in their mother tongue, such as Hindi, for the formal greeting and the final greeting, but doing so is not crucial.

In terms of food and entertaining, it's mostly taken for granted that people generally partake of vegetarian food for a business meeting. If a business meeting is to close a deal, it is usually closed in a five-star hotel.

In terms of gift-giving, guests are generally treated with much reverence and importance. But at a first meeting, nobody expects a gift. Again, if the nature of the business involves fast-moving consumer goals, a soap or shampoo dealer might want to give a gift of memorabilia. It depends on the product that is being sold or transacted.

Relationship-building is important in India, as is making contact through someone already known.

During negotiations in India, people sometimes take things too personally even when they clearly know that it is a professional negotiation. Be careful not to get too emotional over your negotiations. Be patient as you await the contract since, in business, things move at a very slow pace in India.

Contracts need to be written but the rule in India is that there are no contracts, only trust. Their word is their bond.

Things not to do in India include dwelling on the contrasts between the rich and poor. And don't eat meat in front of a vegetarian.

## ITALY

In Italy both men and women greet each other with two kisses, one on each cheek. The standard handshake is becoming the norm for business meetings, especially in the north, but you still need to take each situation as it arises. After a few meetings and getting to know people, however, salutations quickly turn to the traditional method of two kisses. Contrary to popular belief, pinching is no longer accepted.

Italian is the official language but most businesspeople, especially in the major cities like Rome, Milan, and Venice, will speak fluent English. When you get outside the major cities and into the smaller towns, however, English is not heard as often until you go to a four- or five-star international hotel.

Peter Farina is the President of ItalyMONDO! LLC, a company based in both the United States and Italy that conducts on-site genealogical research and Heritage Tours to Italian locations for those exploring their Italian heritage. He says that in America, business deals are made "on the golf course." In Italy, they are made in "bars" or in restaurants. Considering that food is synonymous with Italy and the Italian culture, this is no surprise. However, note that most bars are more like cafés. To chat informally about a subject, the first thing said is often *Andiamo al bar*, "let's go to the bar."

Farina says that for more serious conversations, it's often common practice to go out to lunch. Everyone pays for themselves except when hosting a prospective client; then, as in America, common practice is for the host to pay for lunch. Farina says that many Italian businessmen joke, and lament, about meetings with American businessmen who invite them out to lunch and then expect at the end that the tab will be split among the table. In Italy, if you invite someone, you pay.

Gifts are not common but if someone throws a party of any sort, it's the custom for a guest to bring a small *pensiero*, or gift.

Italy has a strong cash culture so it can be difficult to find businesses outside of cities and tourist destinations that accept certain credit cards.

In business, relationship-building generally is based on meeting face to face or phone calls rather than an over reliance on e-mails.

Ethics can present a challenge in Italy, but your best course of action is to follow those principles that are right for you. You can be aware that kickbacks or bribes can be accepted, particularly in the south, but that doesn't mean you have to follow those behaviors. Farina points out that the attitude in terms of business negotiations may be a "what's in it for me" approach. He says tactics being used when dealing with government officials, contractors, or public contracts might be considered corruption in another culture. If you are not allowed to offer kickbacks or cash incentives, let that be known and don't take it personally if that is expected of you.

But Farina is quick to point out that he does not take part in those practices or support it either. He says, "I have found success in simply standing my ground and saying 'no.' People can respect a strong character."

There is a saying in Italy, *C'e sempre domain*, which means "there is always tomorrow." One should be prepared to wait on many things, especially those that that involve government offices or banks.

## JAPAN

Until recently, the 128 million people of Japan were the premiere business force to reckon with. Although they are having business challenges as an economy, especially since the earthquake and tsunami of March 2011, this is still a country with enormous business potential.

The Japanese speak calmly and rarely use gestures to make a point. Although English is spoken by most businessmen and women, especially at higher level management, you may still want to have a translator with you to avoid missing the nuances in your discussions if you are only relying on English.

In general, the Japanese are very formal and polite in business situations. Joking is not part of their culture.

Food is an important part of doing business in Japan and salaried men often value drinking with their colleagues as a way of getting to know them better. It's even said that it is more difficult to get a promotion or to get a contract if you can't drink, especially for a man. (Recently, more young men don't drink, though.) A typical place for business entertaining would be a fancy bar—possibly even an erotic club—or a karaoke bar.

As noted previously, gift giving is an important part of doing business in Japan.

The negotiating style is very polite and cautious. Japanese will take time to reach a consensus. They don't appreciate aggressive and pushy behavior. It is a very group-oriented society where you're always considered part of a team.

When drawing up a contract, the Japanese appreciate "humble and modest." It's a common phrase to say "No, I'm not enough at all. I need more and more learning" when someone gives you a compliment even if you think you're good.

If you want to avoid committing a *faux pas*, do not bring up World War II, or Hiroshima. In Japan, it is almost always, "work first, money last." Sticking to a money issue in the first place could even be a taboo because you will give the impression of being too greedy.

Japanese people have a very strong work ethic. They think work is a virtue even if you don't get paid. They basically work not only for money but for satisfying themselves psychologically.

They value non-material things, like work, more than money. In Japan, many companies force their employees to retire at 60 unless the employee is an executive. But the idea of an early retirement is not something to look forward to because the majority of Japanese men want to work as long as possible.

## MEXICO

According to Leah D. Cochran of Atlanta-based Glocal Consulting, in Mexico, they like to get to know you as a person before doing business, to see who you are and how serious you are. In Mexico it is important to do business on their terms. If you go there on a whirlwind and expect things to get done, you can literally sit for hours waiting for the person you're going to meet. I recommend never doing more than two or three meetings a day. A meeting can last thirty minutes to two hours. It depends on how many times you've already met as well as on the situation and on the person.

For the most part, negotiations are done in a calm way.

Avoid discussing politics, religion, and if you do discuss sports, like football (which is soccer in the U.S.) try not to express too strong an opinion about which team you cheer for.

As Cochran points out, Mexicans are well aware of the violence that plagues their cities and has threatened the lives of their businessmen and women and their families. But you might want to avoid bringing that up in business meetings, and instead, only discuss it with the local agent you are working with. If you go there on your own, you might want to hire a driver or bodyguard. Check out the website for the U.S. Embassy and the State Department and see if there are any new warnings about specific cities or locations where you might be traveling. Kidnapping has become a growth industry in parts of Mexico.

## NETHERLANDS

The 16.5 million people of the Netherlands are very literate and although Dutch is the official language, the business community speaks fluent English.

Your business discussion will most likely take place in an office but you can certainly move it to a restaurant setting. Gift giving is not necessary or expected in doing business in the Netherlands. However, if you are invited to someone's home, bring flowers or a bottle of liquor.

Plan to be on time when you have business or social meetings. Be careful about being too pushy in business. Take your time. Avoid the *faux pas* of confusing Belgians with the Dutch.

Terms that are used to describe the Dutch include "straightforward" and "direct." Those traits are what they expect when doing business with you, not deviousness or manipulation. But without being underhanded, you might be more successful if you find a way to have your Dutch business partner or associate think that something you want to achieve was their idea and you are going along with it.

Having a referral to those with whom you plan to do business, and praiseworthy letters of recommendation, will go far in helping you win over a potential client or customer.

# NEW ZEALAND

Smaller in population than its neighbor Australia, the four million residents of New Zealand are part of a much more rural country with a slightly more relaxed approach to business in general than the Aussies. The majority of New Zealanders are of European descent, with the first settlers arriving in the 1600s, followed by a bigger wave commencing with Captain James Cook's voyage of 1768-71. New Zealanders are sensitive about the indigenous Mauri who are somewhat akin to the Native American Indians in the United States whose land was taken from them by the European settlers. In recognition of the importance of the Mauri people, in 1987 their language became the second official language in New Zealand. The first is English—with 4% of the population speaking Mauri.

New Zealand mainly consists of two islands: the South Island and the North Island. If you are doing business with New Zealand over the Internet or traveling there for business meetings, you would be expected to know what island you are visiting—Christchurch is on the South Island and the cities of Auckland and Wellington are on the North Island—just as you would be expected to know that Los Angeles is on the West Coast and New York City is on the East Coast of the United States.

New Zealanders are blunt about their opinions in business. They will tell you what they think and not apologize for their views even if it means they do not choose to work with you.

Punctuality is important in business; being late can start a meeting on the wrong foot and you may have a hard time turning the bad feelings around.

# PORTUGAL

Portuguese people speak many languages but they are very happy when a foreigner tries to speak Portuguese with them. In Portugal, a country of about 11 million, with Lisbon its largest city with a population in the city and the surrounding suburbs of close to 2 million, business entertaining is done in restaurants. A unique food to Portugal, that is very popular, is *bacalhau,* which means "cod."

Adriana Navarro is a businesswoman who grew up in Brazil but who lives in Spain and deals extensively with Portugal. She says that business people greet each other with kisses.

It is very common to give gifts in business in Portugal, mostly at the end of the year.

In terms of relationship-building, people generally try to have a long-term personal relationship and to mix the personal with the business.

In their negotiations, Portuguese people are very passionate and can promise you many things that in the end they may not actually accomplish. It's very important to avoid leaving things in an informal way. It is much better to sign contracts to avoid any misunderstandings of problems later on.

*Faux pas* to avoid: Confusing Portugal with Brazil. As Navarro points out: "Portugal is a country that used to live in the past. Now, with the European Union, things are very different. But try to talk to old people in Portugal and you see the Portuguese soul."

## RUSSIA

In Russia, most gestures are similar to U.S., but the "OK" sign is considered vulgar. Hands in the pockets means disrespect. When you greet someone in Russia for business, handshakes are the rule, but it is considered gallant for men to kiss a woman's hand. (It is not actually a kiss but a bending over the hand with lips almost touching.) Hugs are usually reserved for friends, and they are accompanied by three kisses alternating on the cheeks.

In terms of language, in business, English is spoken with foreigners although Russian is the national language.

Russians like to entertain with lavish dinners consisting of a multitude of appetizers, called *zakuski*, soup course, a fish course and a meat course, as well as dessert. A meal often called "tea" is served in the afternoon, and can consist of numerous sweet and savory courses along with the tea. Vodka is the national drink. It is served ice cold, and is not sipped or mixed. It is customary for guests to sit around the table and take turns with their host in raising shot glasses of vodka and giving a toast, after which the vodka is downed in one motion. The third toast traditionally is to the ladies. A simple toast is *Na Zdarovye,* which means "To your health."

As noted before, Communist rule ended in Russia in 1990 but there are still signs of it since it controlled the country for almost 100 years. The new Russia is still sorting out what it is, and getting business done requires patience and being sure you are dealing with honest people.

Relationship-building is one way to foster your trust that you are negotiating with a reliable person and company.

Avoid bringing up the high crime rates in the major cities or any of the dark periods in Russia's past, including the "cold war," since they are trying to forge a new path in business and in their international reputation.

## SOUTH KOREA

South Korea, which is also known as the Republic of Korea, is a country of 49 million. It has its own unique culture and business style; do not confuse it with those who live and work in Taiwan, mainland China, or Japan.

A Korean may greet you with a handshake and a slight bow.

At every business meeting, your business card is important. If possible have your card printed in English on one side and in Korean on the back. Your name, company, and title should be clear since this will indicate if you are at the correct status to be having a meeting.

Korean is the official language. Although English is a language that is usually communicated easily through e-mail exchange, do not assume the person you are meeting with will be comfortable speaking English with you.

Business entertaining is more likely to be conducted at a restaurant than at home.

When you initially meet, you might want to bring an inexpensive but useful gift, such as a promotional item with your company's name on it. A gift from your region of your country of origin can also be a welcome business gift. Gifts will not be opened in front of you so do not take that personally. It's an extension of the reluctance of a Korean person to say "no." Because of that reluctance, be careful how you word things in business. For example, if you have been patiently waiting for a new contract, you could say "When do you expect the contract to be ready?" rather than asking, "Will you have the contract by Thursday?" which would require a "yes" or "no" answer. Since it's hard for them to say "no," they may say nothing or even "yes" whether the contract will be ready by that date or not.

Building trust and communicating with someone who is familiar with the culture and language of South Korea is vital. It is therefore in your best interest to find a local contact with whom you will develop a mutually respectful business relationship. He or she will represent you and your goods or services and negotiate with the buyers or vendors on your behalf. If you do not have a local contact, at least get an introduction through someone who knows the party you wish to meet. That will help to lessen the suspicion about who you are to do business with.

Work out the terms you want with your intermediary. He or she will then negotiate with the Korean counterpart on your behalf. Koreans tend to be expert negotiators using carefully crafted strategies, like choreographed chair-throwing described in detail in the book, *Global Negotiation: The New Rules* by Requejo and Graham (referenced in the Bibliography). Such actions might seem spontaneous but are actually planned and orchestrated to throw off the other party.

Drafts of a written contract are shared with both parties and once there is an agreement on the terms, one party will sign, followed by the other. Contractual terms are expected to be honored.

Here are some *faux pas* to avoid: Confusing Koreans, Japanese, Taiwanese, and Chinese people, languages, and cultures; and discussing the North Korean situation, communism, or socialism.

Religious affiliations in South Korea are almost equally divided between Christians (49%) and Buddhists (47%) so do not make snap assumptions about the religious beliefs of someone living and working in South Korea.

## SPAIN

In Spain, be prepared to have your handshake followed by a kiss on both cheeks, especially if you have an established business relationship with someone.

Spanish is the official language and although in the major cities English is a second language, taxi drivers and storekeepers may not know it. The Spanish will not be offended or make fun of you if you try to speak some Spanish. They will be flattered that you are trying to learn their language. So learn a couple of simple phrases to start and end your business meeting, such as *coma esta*? (How are you?)

The Spanish, like the Italians, take their food very seriously. They also don't want to be rushed when they do have a meal with a business associate so plan to have at least an hour or two for a midday lunch or a couple of hours for an evening meal, with dinner not being served until 9 or 10 at night. It is a sign of respect to order Spanish food when you are in Spain. If you are uncertain about what a dish is on the menu because you cannot read Spanish, you can ask your host or the waiter to describe the dish to you. You can also always say that you will order the same dishes that your host or hostess is ordering.

Bringing a gift to an initial business meeting could be viewed with suspicion. Only bring a gift when your business relationship has developed to a point that it is a comfortable exchange. If you are going to give someone a gift for business, the Spanish would prefer a gift that is more than just an imprinted promotional item although an object in good taste, like a nice pen or a pad holder, with the company name imprinted in a subtle way, would be acceptable.

Having a local representative who can introduce you to the right buyers, companies, or vendors is essential. Choose this representative carefully since some may require exclusivity and changing this person or firm for another will be viewed in a negative way.

In business, the Spanish are not confrontational and they do not like to say "no." Rather than negotiate till an agreement is reached, they may just pull back and shelve the deal unless you do something to try to get a discussion going so a compromise can be reached. A written contract is expected with all the terms spelled out.

Here are some *faux pas* to avoid: trying to order Mexican dishes at a restaurant in Spain instead of food native to Spain; or making disparaging comments about the national pastime, the bullfight.

The pace of life and what type of dress is expected is quite different in two of the major cities for business, Barcelona and Madrid. Barcelona is more like Los Angeles in that the climate is hotter and although women in business may still wear business suits, men may dress in more of a business casual way, especially if they work for a smaller company. Madrid is more like Manhattan; it is cooler and it also tends to be more formal in attire.

## TAIWAN

Taiwan, with its 23 million people, is a country that prides itself on its work ethic and business savvy. When you greet someone in Taiwan, exchanging business cards will follow shaking hands.

Abel Zalcberg, co-founder and CEO of OFM, Inc., an office and school furniture manufacturer, distributor, and wholesaler, has been doing business in Taiwan for twenty years including regular trips there. He says there is a certain way of giving someone your business card in Taiwan. It is presented with two hands, then a little bow, which is usually reciprocated.

Taiwanese and Mandarin are spoken. From a language point of view, very few speak English, especially in the smaller towns, but many companies have salespeople who are hired to speak English or to translate for the owner, who might not speak English, or to make it easier for the business owners to understand.

Taiwanese people eat a lot of vegetables, rice, and fish, and rarely eat meat. For the most part, they will ask you, "Do you like fish? We'll go for fish tonight." They are not fast food oriented.

Entertaining for business is done in a restaurant, and in private rooms. After dinner, there is entertainment. They have Karaoke parlors where you go and sing with them and there are escorts there to sing with you.

Whenever someone from Taiwan comes to the United States for business, they always bring a gift. When visiting Taiwan for business, out of three visits a year, gifts will be brought just once. Gifts might be a writing instrument, a belt, a scarf, promotional items from the company, or golf balls.

Abel Zalcberg points out that their political system is always in conflict with China because China wants Taiwan to become a Chinese state and Taiwan wants to be independent.

Zalcberg shares that he has observed in the twenty years that he has been doing business in Taiwan, it has become commercialized. Now you see Taiwanese either driving Mercedes, Lexus, BMWs, or riding bicycles or scooters. It's a very divergent culture: you either have money, or you don't.

The typical business model is that you establish a long-term business relationship that is more like a partnership.

Zalcberg notes that until the Taiwanese get to know you, there is very little negotiating. They don't trust you yet so you have to have a letter of credit that has guaranteed payments by a bank or they ask for a deposit with the order and the balance when they ship the order.

Once they trust you, however, you can ask for some dating meaning that you can ask for thirty, sixty, or ninety days dating but you'll still need a letter of credit.

In his two decades of business with twelve different furniture factories in Taiwan, Abel Zalcberg says he's never had a written contract. However, you may be more comfortable with a standard written contract.

*Faux pas* to avoid: don't refuse a meal the first time you are invited. To the Taiwanese, that is one of the most important friendship gestures that they make. After you've been with them for six, seven, or ten trips, you can say no because you're not feeling well or you have to get up early, but the first time someone invites you to eat with them, you'd better go.

## UNITED KINGDOM

In terms of gestures, the United Kingdom is similar to U.S. However, gesticulating while speaking is considered impolite, so it is best to limit any hand or arm gestures. For a business greeting, handshakes are the rule. If by chance you get to meet the Queen of England, however, you should bow or curtsey. Titles are very important. If you expect to be introduced to a member of the nobility, be sure you know how to address that person: "My Lord," or "My Lady," or "Your Grace" for hereditary nobles. You should not address these individuals as "you" but speak to them in the third person, as in "Would Your Ladyship like a beverage?"

Some words mean different things in the UK. For example, to "knock up" means to call for someone, underpants are "knickers" and the elevator is the "lift" and if you are ordering in food for a meeting it is called "take away" not "take out."

Food and entertaining practices are similar to U.S. "Black tie" means formal dinner jackets for men and gowns for women. Stand up for a formal toast: the first toast of the evening at a reception or formal dinner party is "to the Queen" or "to the health of the Queen."

It is not customary to exchange gifts in business interactions. Even though the United Kingdom is part of the EU (European Union), they still use their own currency, UK Pounds Sterling £ in bills and coins.

Their political system is a monarchy, with the Queen as the titular head of state, but the real political power in the hands of the Prime Minister and his or her Cabinet.

The British legal system is based on common law, and is the basis for the U.S. system. Courts are independent. One peculiarity of the UK system is its libel laws, which make it relatively easy to secure a judgment against those who deliberately print false information about you. This has led to numerous lawsuits by celebrities against British newspapers. The British take their privacy very seriously. They also take their monarchy very seriously so you should not say anything disparaging about their century-old traditions, or all the hoopla around the latest Royal family gossip.

The UK has been a global trading nation since the fifteenth century so the business community is experienced in dealing with other nations. It does not require pre-existing relationships in order to do business. While British business people can drive a hard bargain, they tend to work toward compromise.

The British tend to be more formal than Americans so it is considered a *faux pas* in business to be too informal. You should not call people by their first name unless invited to do so. When it comes to other related business matters, put your best foot forward including promptly responding to invitations, and being on time to dinner parties or meetings.

For business dress, it would be appropriate to wear a suit with a tie for men, and a suit or dress for women although pants suits are acceptable as well. Dark colors, except in summer, are preferable.

## UNITED STATES

In the United States, types of greetings can vary greatly based on what part of the country you're in and the level of intimacy in the relationship. Those in the East tend to be more formal than those in the South, Midwest, or West. If it is a new business meeting, it will be very formal, with just a handshake. After business associates know each other, women may hug or kiss each other but it is safest to just shake hands in business.

Most Americans are uncomfortable if there is too little personal space between them. They don't want to stand too close or too far apart.

English is spoken in business unless of course the business is with one of the diverse populations in the United States and they are new to the U.S. and do not yet speak English fluently. Unlike other foreign countries, especially in Europe, a very small segment of the population speaks a second language fluently. Those who are first or second generation immigrants may still speak the language of the country from which they emigrated, and a certain percentage of Spanish-speaking Americans are fluent in both English and Spanish. But, in general, the typical American is not known for being fluent in many languages. Younger businessmen and women, however, are learning Mandarin, Russian, Portuguese, Spanish, and Arabic so they can do business more easily around the world in those countries without needing a translator.

In terms of food and entertaining for business in the United States, each of the major divisions of the country has its own cuisine. When doing business in that part of the country, you might want to get the dishes that are distinctive such as TexMex in the West, Southern cooking in the South, meat and potatoes and apple pie in the Midwest, steak in Manhattan, or New England clam chowder and New York cheesecake in the northeast and New England.

Entertaining for business can be done in an office or over a meal including breakfast meetings, which can start as early as 7 or 8 a.m. and could be held in a restaurant or in a hotel suite if someone is staying in a five-star hotel. Business lunches are still popular but are a lot more scaled back than in the days when no one was watching their expense accounts. Discussing business over drinks or dinner is also acceptable. Being invited to someone's home for dinner or for a business function, like a holiday party, is usually done if the business relationship has moved to a certain point of familiarity—although it might be done for the first meeting if someone is coming from a far away country.

Business gifts are a very tricky consideration in the U.S. because of all the political scandals tied to gift giving and accusations of influence peddling. In this regard, the U.S. has a very different stance than many other countries. Some U.S. government agencies have very strict policies against any kind of a gift, let alone money, even at the holidays. It is definitely considered poor form to send someone a gift in business if you are in the midst of negotiations, but once the deal is done, a gift, as long as it's not too expensive, could be a nice way to show gratitude for the business you have concluded or are commencing. Some companies have strict policies about how much money can be spent on a business gift, within the company or to others, with a range of spending allowed, depending on the status of the employee, from as low as $10 or $25 to as much as $100 or more for a senior executive. Rules are much stricter for government and public than private sector companies but you still need to be careful that your gift will be appreciated and that it won't backfire. Something that reflects the town, city, state, or country where you are from, or the business that you are representing, could be a welcome gift. Gifts should be wrapped and there should be a card or note included.

The political system is a democracy with a president elected every four years. There is a two party system—Democrats and Republicans—representing distinct perspectives with a growing number of citizens considering themselves independents.

In business, and in relationship building in general, it is very important to have an entre to whatever business or company you want to do business with. The stakes in business are so high that it takes time to build trust. Once that trust is developed, however, you may find companies wanting to work with you for years and years rather than start with someone new and unproven. In some industries, however, it is more of a cost issue and building relationships is not as pivotal. So it depends on the type of business and work that you are doing. But even if a friend, business associate, or family member helps to open up the door to doing business in the U.S., it will be necessary to prove yourself to maintain the business.

In terms of negotiating style and contracts, Americans have grown used to having everything in writing even if they start off the business with a handshake. It is important to read every contract carefully and if the language is unclear or too technical, hire a lawyer to read it over for you. Put in the contract what you will do if the contract is breached—possibly having mediation or arbitration as an alternative to a law suit.

When doing business in or with the United States, the *faux pas* to avoid include racist, sexist, or ethnic jokes or slurs, bringing up the Civil War, discussing politics, religion, or how much money someone makes in a business meeting especially if you've just met.

The U.S. is very much a results-oriented culture. Business hours are traditionally nine to five but in some businesses, like the world of international finance, law, or the creative arts, people can work from dawn until after nine at night. Some Americans are sensitive about the fact that most of them do not get the same four or more weeks of vacations as their European counterparts. American women have achieved more equality in business than in other cultures but there are still only 5.1% of the top executive spots in the U.S. filled by women compared to only 1 to 3 percent globally, but that is still an increase from 1996 when it was just 2.4%.

# CHAPTER 5

# *Doing Business Globally Without Leaving Home*

During times of economic challenge, budget-conscious companies large and small tend to trim back spending on international travel and rely instead on virtual meetings either over the Internet, phone or by video conferencing. If you are just starting your company, or lack the funds to travel to foreign lands, there still are plenty of ways to grow your business globally without ever leaving your home or office.

Technology has made communicating over the Internet or by phone not only more affordable but more dynamic as well. With a video camera and Skype you can both see and hear the person you're talking to. Even in good times, communicating by phone and the Internet will still be integral channels for business communication.

## OVER THE PHONE

Despite the convenience and cost-effectiveness of using e-mail while conducting business internationally, communicating by phone continues to be an essential counterpart. Unfortunately, calling internationally is not always that simple or that inexpensive unless you and the person you are calling have computer access to Skype, which may be free. Another concern is figuring out whether you might be calling at an inconvenient time since you are likely spanning several time zones. If you are on the East Coast of the United States and calling India, there is not only a nine-hour difference, but you are also into another day.

You may have language barriers that were not as apparent when you were communicating through e-mail. A colleague may be able to communicate clearly in writing, but not speak English that well. Or, as noted earlier, accents can make it difficult to understand the spoken English.

A Scotland-based employee of a large American engineering company told a teleconference organizer that he could not understand what team members from Tennessee were saying. Similarly, his American counterparts said the man's Scottish brogue was incomprehensible over the phone, although interestingly, they could understand him in person. There are ways around language challenges. You can follow up the call with an e-mail to restate what was said in the call. Or you can have interpreters or translators in on the call to clarify any misunderstandings due to different dialects and accents.

## USING THE "MUTE" BUTTON

It is easy to forget that you are conducting a business discussion when the other party is not actually facing you. The temptation to multi-task or hold side-bar conversations could lead you to overlook important points in the discussion, or blurt out comments that are better kept private. This is where using the "mute" button becomes invaluable. One American executive who was in the middle of a legal maneuver with German colleagues over the telephone startled her colleagues when they heard her snap the words "shut up!" while still on the line. The Germans were later mollified when the embarrassed executive explained that she had been addressing her two Labrador retrievers, who were barking and throwing themselves against her patio door.

The sounds of paper rustling, breathing, or coffee being sipped are annoying distractions, especially on conference calls. So when you are not talking, hit the mute button, or at least take the call off speakerphone, especially if there are other distracting sounds, like family pets, or the sawing of trees outside the window of your home office. Of course, it goes without saying that you have to remember to take your phone off mute before you start talking again; otherwise no one will hear what you have to say.

## PLAN AHEAD BY CREATING
## A WRITTEN AGENDA

Because it is not always easy to communicate by telephone across language, geographic and cultural barriers, a useful approach to such conversations is to prepare an agenda in advance of the meeting. Being prepared also includes:

- Making sure that the time for the conversation is convenient to all parties.

- E-mailing the agenda for the discussion in advance to allow all parties to prepare.

- Establishing ground rules for the conversation, i.e., who will participate and, if using a speakerphone or taping, obtaining permission from all relevant parties.

- Speaking slowly and clearly, and avoiding colloquialisms or abbreviations, unless you are sure all parties understand them.

- Following up telephone conversations with an e-mail or written memorandum covering the key points discussed and understandings reached, which are shared with all participants.

- Avoiding discussions of confidential or proprietary material unless you have a confidentiality or non-disclosure agreement in place, and have secure telephone facilities for the conversation.

- Having an interpreter or translator on the call (who is a company employee or who has signed a non-disclosure agreement) to help with any language, dialect and accent challenges so that everyone is clear about what is being said in your business call.

*If you find that you need a single word or phrase translated while you are on the telephone, the Internet offers a quick fix. You can use online word translation services, such as www.freetranslation.com or www.translation.google.com, which offer immediate assistance in understanding unfamiliar words or phrases.*

If you find that you need a single word or phrase translated while you are on the telephone, the Internet offers a quick fix. You can use online word translation services, such as www.freetranslation.com or www.translation. google.com, which offer immediate assistance in understanding unfamiliar words or phrases. Keep in mind that such software-based translations are not capable of making intelligent distinctions among multiple meanings of words. Therefore, they are not recommended for accurate translations of complex texts. They can, however, be useful in clarifying a word or phrase that may not be readily understood in a telephone conversation. If you have immediate access to the Internet, this can be a savior.

## INTERNATIONAL
## PHONE ETIQUETTE

If you are the one placing the call, be aware of what time it is going to be for the person you are calling. If you are unsure, use a free online website, such as www.timeanddate.com to figure it out. Put the city you want to call into the search box and it will find the time for you.

If you are making an unscheduled call to someone and you get him or her on the phone, start the conversation by asking, "Is this a good time to talk?" You could be intruding. Don't automatically assume that it's a good time to talk just because you got someone on the phone.

Whether you're in Manhattan calling Sydney, Australia or in Chicago calling Paris, after you say hello and share a few pleasantries, get on with the reason for your call. You can mention the weather as an ice breaker or something to say in between discussion points, but for business calls, stay on point and message. Keep the conversation clear and short. Avoid rambling. You should, however, show an interest in the other person by asking about him or her while not probing too deeply into their personal lives. Since you are calling internationally, it is certainly acceptable to ask or comment about global issues that you both might find interesting and wish to share your opinions.

Have a specific agenda for your call even if your only reason is just to say "hello" and to network. Be ready with something important to discuss, such as: "I'm wondering if you got those materials that I mailed to you?" or

"Have you decided if you're attending the trade show next month?" Say something other than "I just called to say 'hello,'" unless of course you have a well-established personal relationship with this global business colleague, customer, client, or associate.

Take notes of your phone conversation as well as the time of day you called. If this seemed to be a good time for the other person to talk, it will serve as a nice reference point for when you call again.

Even though it may be easier to put someone on speakerphone, the etiquette is to ask permission first, and also to be cognizant that this might disturb those around you if you are in an open office or cubicle.

As you wind down your international phone call, make it clear what the next steps will be: will you follow-up with an e-mail, a letter, or another call?

Before you get off the phone, politely thank him or her for the time on the phone.

## RECEIVING THE CALL

If you are the one who is receiving the call and this is not a good time for you to talk, tell that to the caller right away, even if the person is calling from another country, and then politely ask to schedule a better time for another call. If the call had been scheduled in advance apologize if you are now unable to talk and ask if you could call them back as soon as you complete whatever task is keeping you from the call. Don't let the caller talk for so long that when you interrupt to say it is not a good time to talk that it sounds as if you are cutting him or her off because you don't find what is being said useful or interesting. Since this is a business call, you should always be pleasant and upbeat, even if you are busy or in a bad mood.

Determine as quickly as possible who the person is, why he or she is calling, and if you are the right person to handle this call. If you aren't, suggest someone else, explain why, and provide that person's contact information. Even if the caller is a total stranger or someone that you feel is on a different level business-wise, be friendly yet business-like because you are a reflection of your company or agency.

Try to be aware of how much time you are spending on the phone. Keep a record of who you spoke with and the contact information of the caller so it will be easier to follow-up later.

## MOBILE PHONE INTERNATIONAL PROTOCOLS

There are a number of mobile phone protocol concerns to consider when doing business internationally.  For example, it is universally impolite to have your phone go off during a meeting, unless you are expecting a call from someone that directly pertains to that meeting. To avoid interruption, either turn off your phone, or put it on vibrate during the meeting.

If you are constantly having trouble with poor cell phone reception, you may need to invest in a new cell phone or change service providers to one that offers better coverage so you do not jeopardize your business or career. When traveling by train, always respect the "quiet car" rule and move elsewhere before talking on your cell phone.

If you have a policy of not dealing with business calls after hours, and you answer your cell phone, as long as you made the decision to answer your phone, still be professional and agreeable. But quickly find out who is calling you and why, and if you prefer to adhere to your "no business calls after business hours" ask when you can return the call. Just because someone is calling you internationally does not mean you have to take the call if you are asleep or busy. An exception of course would be in an emergency situation. You should also take the call if your boss or an important business partner or customer is on the line because putting off that type of conversation may not be in your best interest.

If you are willing to answer your cell phone at any time, or if your cell phone is used mainly for business, always answer it in a professional manner.

## PHONE SCAMS

International telephone fraud is a growing concern for many companies and entrepreneurs. These attempts, sometimes known as "phone phishing," have become increasingly frequent and more sophisticated. The term "phone phishing" defines an effort to deceive employees or business men or women into providing proprietary or private information about their company or key employees for the purpose of illicit financial gain. The caller may fish (or "phish") for information including but not limited to:

- Names and direct phone numbers of key company executives
- Details surrounding information technology (IT) security procedures
- Financial, sales, or accounting data

The caller may pose as a vendor or even a company employee in order to obtain this information which might be used to try to gain an unfair business advantage by having this insider information.

One of the best ways to defeat a possible phishing attempt is to take your time, carefully question a caller's identity, and demand verification when asked for information. Telephone con artists are skilled at sounding credible. If you receive a call from someone claiming to work for an institution and requesting information, contact the institution directly and ask if the company has initiated the inquiry.

Verify any "call-back" numbers given by the caller with an outside source, such as directory assistance or the institution's website. Do not discuss confidential or proprietary information on the phone unless you have positively identified the caller as legitimate. For example, companies conducting business with the IRS do not call to request or verify confidential information. If you receive such a call, it is more than likely a "phishing" attempt. In all cases where you believe you have received a phishing call, contact your supervisor, information technology representative, or security department immediately.

## TELECONFERENCING

While the telephone has long been used as a shortcut to communicating with foreign business contacts and organizations, the technologies fueling teleconferencing and videoconferencing have radically changed the landscape. Teleconferencing can be a wonderful way to be in two places at once, especially when the distances are vast and the time and resources to be in that location are formidable. Compare the cost and time involved of having a discussion by teleconference with someone in the United States and five people in five different cities around the world versus getting on a plane and flying to all those locations, not to mention the cost of ground transportation, meals, and hotels.

However, while teleconferencing may be less expensive than flying around the world, it is really just a telephone call that is being accessed by two or more individuals and is not an equal substitute for the in-person meeting. It also can be difficult to tell voices apart if the teleconference involves several people, especially of the same gender, and if their voices sound similar. Without offending anyone, you might have a rule that someone has to say his or her name before speaking so everyone does not have to constantly ask, "Who was that just speaking?"

Even if it is just a teleconference and not a videoconference, you might suggest that each individual make available a photograph of himself or herself on the computer as people speak. That could help to make the conversation seem a bit more personalized even though it is basically just the voices and words that are being shared.

There are a number of logistical and auditory challenges of a teleconference, including potential language differences. Therefore, it may be useful to have someone offer to create a transcript of the conversation to be made available afterwards to everyone who was on the call. Offer each teleconference attendee who participated in the conversation the opportunity to make any corrections to his or her statements, making sure that statements attributed to a specific individual were, indeed, that person's comments and not the comments of another.

A teleconferencing industry has developed to address this growing international communications method. One teleconferencing service based in Birmingham, Alabama, Moreson Conferencing, enables the companies who subscribe to it to have a permanent conferencing number that is the same, whatever country they are calling.

## VIDEO CONFERENCING

As companies trim their travel budgets, videoconferencing becomes popular as a cost-effective link between customers and suppliers or management teams in distant corners of the world. It enables them to make instant decisions on fast-breaking developments. In the run up to the 1999 celebrations of the 50th Anniversary of the North Atlantic Treaty Organization (NATO), it became clear that travel to the sixteen member capitals and coordination among them was a logistical nightmare. So the U.S. State Department began organizing videoconferences with diplomats from the other member states and the prospective new members.

A video teleconference has the advantage of bringing all the stakeholders to the table at one time, sharing information on a real-time basis, solving problems that arise, and making collective decisions instantaneously. Each participant has to have "secure" or eavesdropping-proof facilities, and highly sensitive issues are reserved for off-line and private discussions, but the procedures have worked so well that the State Department and other U.S. Government agencies now routinely use video teleconferencing for conference planning as well as for other negotiations.

A key advantage of video teleconferencing is that it enables the participants to read "body language" which at times can be more important than spoken language. Watching a negotiating partner drop his or her eyes during a conversation or shake his or her head "no" is as telling as the words being said. This is especially true when cultural or language differences are factored in.

As has been noted before, in some Southeast Asian societies, cultural norms make it difficult for one party to actually say "no" when dealing with a business partner. Watching that person turn aside or fidget during a conversation provides a strong indicator that he or she is reluctant to agree, and that another approach is needed. Similarly, for those speaking a language that is not native to them, there may be nuances that are lost in a simple exchange of e-mails or in a telephone conversation but which can be more easily picked up in a videoconference.

## PRACTICAL CONSIDERATIONS

Even if it is your employer who picks up the phone bill when you are traveling for business, it is often a shock to discover that you have a $1,000 mobile or cell phone bill for just two weeks abroad.

One way to keep this cost down is to rent an international cell phone in the country where you're traveling. The rental phone will enable you to get free incoming calls; you only pay for outgoing calls and you can pay in advance for a set amount of money. Once you reach that amount, you either stop using the phone or prepay more. But at least you do not have to worry about returning home to an astronomical cell phone bill.

You can look into buying a cell phone for as little as $99 that works in 170 countries including the U.S. You can use it to call when you are going to and from the airport if you want to leave your regular cell phone at home. You will get an assigned phone number for the phone which is your own number forever. The service is supposed to be less expensive than using your own cell phone to call internationally because calls are charged per minute without any usage or roaming charges.

Using Skype is another low-cost or free alternative to exorbitant phone bills. (All parties need to have Skype on their computer or smart phone to be able to use it for free.) If you want people to be able to call you even if they lack Skype, you can buy a Skype-in number that costs $60 a year.

Another possible option is something called "Google Voice." (At this writing, Google Voice is available by invitation only, but it could become more accessible soon.) It was created by the company behind the search engine Google.com. Google Voice enables you to get voicemail like an e-mail and transcribe what your voicemail says. You can have low-cost international calls, and you can have one number that rings all of your telephones. Other features include recording phone conversations as well as conducting conference calls.

## CONDUCTING INTERNATIONAL
## BUSINESS OVER THE INTERNET

It has become increasingly common to have a website for your international business. This site could represent a corporate site with actual offices around the world, a small business that is selling products from the site, or the site of an entrepreneur who is offering services internationally.

While I'm not going to go into how to set up a website, there are a number of factors you need to take into account if you plan on doing business internationally. If you are working with a webmaster, make sure you let him or her know that your site needs to be international in scope, and whether you are targeting certain countries or areas or "the world."

Here are some ways to turn your basic website into an international one:

- Have the website translated into the languages of the countries that you are seeking out for business, such as French, Spanish, or Japanese, with the translation done by a trained professional, if possible.

- Alternatively, list the "urls" for translating your website into a variety of languages.

- Include a search box so it is easier to find particular products or services.

- Consider a "text only" option or at least keep photographs and illustrations to a minimum as they slow down the loading time on computers internationally that do not have fast connections.

- Have a currency converter calculator if you are selling products through your website.

- If you ask visitors to provide contact information, include a field for "country" so you can identify the country of origin of your current or potential customers/clients.

- If you do not want to redesign your entire site, consider adding an "international" section where you can include contact information geared to your global visitors as well as how to contact someone by phone, e-mail, or for getting samples or catalogs.

- For direct sales, have the ability to take international credit cards as well as calculate the cost of shipping internationally.

- Make sure your site is "culture sensitive," lacking any flags, language, images, color schemes, or wording that could be seen as controversial in specific countries or parts of the world.

Alison Craig, a Chicago-based image and branding consultant, had a website designer redo her original site so it would be more appealing globally. She decided to redo the whole site for the international market because the logo was too soft and friendly. "It was too casual for the rest of the world," says Alison. "We decided to go to a more traditional business/corporate look in order to look more professional." Her previous site used contrasting colors such as cranberry red and navy blue. She had it changed to shades of gray to make it more "business appropriate." She also built in a translation function so visitors could translate text to Spanish, Chinese, French, and German. The site no longer has graphics on every page, giving it a faster connection. "Visitors can now get the information relatively quickly," she adds. "We're increasing the text a little bit more to compensate for not having so many visuals. We're also making sure we don't have just the traditional American look for my international clients."

## GLOBAL ETIQUETTE WHEN USING E-MAIL

We tend to treat e-mail as an informal method of communication, sometimes using shorthand and symbols to make a point. In business, however, e-mail should be seen in the same light as any other formal business exchange and this is especially important with international business. Here are six principles related to international e-mail communications that will reduce the likelihood that you will offend someone, whatever their culture:

1. Whatever you put in your subject line is going to help determine whether or not your e-mail is opened quickly and read, so choose your words carefully. Avoid any country-specific jargon that might turn off an international reader, and clearly state the business reason for your communication.

2. It is polite to respond to e-mail as soon as possible, preferably immediately, or within 24 hours. If you are pressed for time, acknowledge getting the e-mail by sending a short response explaining why you need more time to send a longer reply.

3. Avoid writing anything confidential or negative in an e-mail since confidentiality cannot be guaranteed and, just as importantly, doing so violates the business protocol rule: praise in writing, but provide feedback, constructive criticism, or reprimands verbally.

4. If you are going out-of-town and do not plan to check your e-mail frequently, or at all, set up an "Auto-responder" which will respond automatically to anyone sending you an e-mail with the information about when you will return as well as the name and contact information for your designee.

5. Avoid sending attached files without permission.

6. Keep your e-mails as brief, clear, and well-written as possible; a business e-mail is not the right situation for writing "stream of consciousness."

## INTERNET SCAMS

As popular as the Internet has become, it is also a rich resource for crooks, con artists, identity thieves and others seeking a quick buck. Who hasn't received an e-mail from Nigeria informing them about an opportunity to make millions? The Nigerian scam became so prevalent that the *Washington Post* published a story in August 2009 about what they termed an "industry."

The *Post* found that con artists in Nigeria were working overtime to take money from naïve Americans and Europeans, even in an economic recession. And they did it by using international e-mails that were cleverly worded appeals for money. They were usually some derivation of asking people to send them a small amount of money with the promise that they would receive a much more substantial amount in return.

It was called the "Nigerian 419" named after the Nigerian criminal code used to designate such activity. All anyone needed to engage in this scam was a laptop with a wireless connection or access to an Internet café. Scammers were earning tens of thousands of dollars a month. They specialized in sending e-mail messages with subject lines like "Urgent Assistance Needed." The messages contained an appeal for money to help someone travel to a bank in a distant land in order to secure vastly greater riches that they would, of course, then share with you. Or they would pose as deposed royalty, needing money to recover their inheritance.

Some scams would inform you that you had won a lottery—even though you had never purchased a ticket. They would try to convince you that entering was automatic and possibly based on a visit to a website. They only needed your bank account information in order to "transfer the winnings" to you.

Another one involves asking you to be their American representative. It almost sounds like a job offer. All you have to do is provide them with your banking information so they can deposit the cash. There are literally dozens of variants of this appeal, all of them bogus.

Whatever the message, do not send money, cash, money orders, or bank checks to persons unknown to you, and do not provide your personal or business banking information, credit card numbers or other business or personal data that can be used to steal your identity over the Internet. Reputable businesses and government agencies will not ask for such information.

The most dangerous scams are the ones that seem legitimate. They are orchestrated in a tricky way. The most common involves so-called "phishing scams." They look like they are coming from your credit card company or a vendor you may have used. They tell you a piece of information is missing from your bank account and you need to provide that information so a deal can go through, or to avoid your account being closed or frozen. Naturally when you provide that information, you are giving it to the scammer, who is never the legitimate business they claim to be, but instead are an illegal operation that is hard to trace. You have made yourself vulnerable to having your company accounts depleted or your identity stolen.

I recently received an e-mail alert from the U.S. Commercial Service advising me of a new international scam where a company from Nigeria tells a vendor that they want to buy $5,000 to $30,000 worth of the vendor's goods. The vendor is told that they have to ship the goods soon, but the shipping costs will be reimbursed. The company pays with a credit card and it all seems legitimate and the vendor who received the e-mail is excited that such a large order has been placed. But as soon as the goods are shipped, the credit card is cancelled. It usually turns out that the credit card was stolen, anyway. The goods are on the way to an untraceable address. In fact, no part of the transaction can be traced. Needless to say, those goods arrive and are taken by the recipient who then sells them without giving any money at all to the original vendor who is out the cost of the goods as well as the shipping costs.

In its booklet, "International Financial Scams," the U.S. Department of State suggests that if you have been the victim of an international scam, "it is best to end all communication with the scam artist, rather than attempt resolution." They add that it is extremely rare for victims to recover lost money. It is also suggested that if you feel threatened in any way, report what's happened to your local police department. If you think you have been the victim of an international scam, you can also report it to www.econsumer.gov which has been created by the Federal Trade Commission to serve as a site providing a place to report complaints about online and related transactions with foreign companies.

## MEETING OR "ENTERTAINING"
## FOREIGN VISITORS

When Americans hear the word *entertaining* they typically think you're talking about a party. But entertaining foreign visitors, in many cultures, simply means that you are having visitors from overseas. You could be entertaining those visitors in your office, at a restaurant, or in your home.

Where you entertain international visitors may have as much to do with what is appropriate for your culture as well as your own personality or logistical issues. For example, your apartment or home may be under renovation, or you may be feeling like the cost of taking ten foreigners out to dinner is outside your company's budget right now. Wherever the entertaining of foreign visitors takes place, remember that the goal of your efforts is to build your international relationship, whether you want it to be just a business relationship or a personal one as well.

Here are some suggestions for making your entertaining of foreign visitors more effective, wherever it takes place. Some of these suggestions may seem obvious but the advice bears repeating since those new to business or less seasoned in entertaining international business visitors may not be familiar with one or more of these basic protocol rules:

- Your visitors have traveled a great distance coming from a foreign country and deserve to have you take the time to make a fuss over them. Even if you did not make the hotel arrangements for your visitor, try to find out where he or she is staying and have a welcome basket of bottled water and some snacks with a nice card or handwritten note delivered to their room in advance of their check-in.

- Whether you have guests in the office, at a restaurant, or in your home, research the culture of the men and women you are entertaining. Find out about any foods or behaviors that they practice so you avoid serving anything that might be offensive. Find out if someone is vegetarian or if you should avoid serving liquor. A dinner at a business associate's home in many countries such as Spain or Denmark can last for several hours so do not arrive with the expectation you can rush off quickly.

- If you can't provide a meal associated with your foreign guest's visit, try to serve them at least a snack, tea, or coffee. If appropriate, include a tour of your offices if this is their first time at your company.

- Be prepared to spend more time with your foreign visitors than you would if your visitors were local. Even with the Internet, and international phone communication so easy, traveling to the office of another from a distant country is still a big deal and should be given the time and attention that accomplishing such a journey still requires.

By being gracious to foreign business visitors when they arrive in your office, you can start off your international business relationship on the right foot. If you have already been doing business together, it will help strengthen the business relationships that you have already begun.

Roberto Angulo, CEO of AfterCollege, Inc., a job searching resource for college students and alumni, told me about how he hosted business visitors from China. He says it made a difference in how his company was perceived by his Chinese business associates and whether they wanted to encourage doing business with him. There were fourteen visitors, and most of them did not speak English. As a result, he says his company needed to constantly wait for someone to translate each sentence to Mandarin. The Chinese like to boast and are proud of the scale at which they do things. For example, Angulo says he showed them the results of a survey his firm did of seven hundred respondents. The Chinese visitors claimed they were planning on conducting a similar survey but with twenty thousand participants. Angulo acknowledged that his survey was not as large as the ones they conduct in China. His humility served him well because not only were his survey results taken seriously, but also opened the doors for business opportunities with various members of the Chinese delegation.

When foreign visitors are in your office, every part of your interaction is still business. Whatever you share should be in the interest of moving your international business and relationship along.

If you really want to shine in the eyes of your foreign visitors, and as long as they have the time for it, ask if they would like you to take them around your town or city, showing them your favorite tourist attractions. This is especially appealing if you work in a travel destination like New York City, Chicago, Los Angeles, New Orleans, Philadelphia, Dallas, or such foreign cities as Madrid, Mumbai, Venice, Paris, Barcelona, Amsterdam, London, or Tokyo. Your visitors will remember you and their visit and what you shared with them in the most positive way, probably even more than they will recall any business discussion or why they met with you in the first place.

Your visitors may initially refuse your offer to show them around because they do not want to look demanding or, if you did not warn them of your plan in advance, they have not allowed enough time for your kind gesture. But ask a second time, showing that you are genuinely sincere. Or, if they will be in town for two or more days, and their schedule allows some time for sightseeing another time, ask them to schedule your sightseeing offer then so you can all make the time available in your schedules. This will honor your guests and give you a chance to show off your hometown. It will also provide an opportunity to get to know each other and within hours build a relationship that could have taken years to achieve.

## IF YOU HAVE A HOME OFFICE

As more and more businesses become virtual offices, whether operating out of the corner of a family room in a house or part of the dining room in an apartment, it is crucial to remember that office protocol still prevails. Even if an international client or customer is willing to visit your home office, you have to consider if that is appropriate for your company or business. If you do have a virtual office and you need to meet with international clients, it may be preferable to instead take them out for a meal or to rent an office, even by the hour, so you can meet them in a more professional setting. Image consultant Alison Craig rents an outside office on a monthly basis from www.regus.com. She likes using their offices because doing so also enables her to access short-term rentals of affiliated office space in locations around the world.

## AT A RESTAURANT OR AT HOME

Entertaining a foreign visitor at a restaurant may work better if you have a home office and prefer to avoid mixing business and your personal life. Even if you work in a plush office setting in Manhattan, your foreign visitors may welcome the chance to be wined and dined at your favorite nearby restaurant. There you will get excellent service and food because you are known to the manager and the chef.

However, even though it is a lot of work to entertain at home, it may better suit your personality and your view of how to treat your foreign guests than going to a commercial establishment. For example, Dick Barnes of The Freelance Group says he has entertained a variety of foreign business guests—Russians, Tajiks, Japanese, and Germans—and did so in his home instead of in a restaurant. He adds that the results were very favorable. But then he has nice home in a pleasant country setting, and his wife is a good cook and hostess. He also had a local driver deliver the business people to his door.

Barnes says it may have been a good deal more trouble than meeting them at a restaurant near their hotel, but the results were worth it. The visits normally ran three to four hours; there was significant time invested as compared to simply going to a restaurant. Meanwhile, his visitors ended up thoroughly enjoying seeing how an American family lived and expressed their appreciation for the experience. The relationships went beyond purely business and have remained so. In most cultures, a personal relationship is the foundation of the business relationship, unlike in the U.S. where we tend to hurry through transactions and make decisions based on the bottom line.

One visitor wished to take a walk through his wooded area, and he and Barnes were both stung by bees. Amazingly, they bonded over the painful experience and the meeting turned out quite successful.

Texas-based artist and designer Pablo Solomon and his wife Beverly entertain for business on their ranch north of Austin. He suggests learning all that you can about your client and the customs of their society. For example, if he's entertaining Islamic clients, he doesn't take them out for margaritas or pork ribs, nor show them any art depicting nude dancers. Pablo says it's important to learn what any society considers to be polite. He once made a fool of himself in the eyes of some French visitors by eating cheese in the wrong sequence in the meal. He also recommends staying away from current events unless your client wants to discuss such items. He noted that in his experience, French, Germans, and Italians love to discuss current events. However, he learned to do more listening than talking.

When entertaining international visitors, it is important for you to dress appropriately. In many cultures, you just do not go to a business meeting dressed casually. Even though you're on home turf and are tempted to go casual, dressing up for your visitor is a sign of respect. Dress as if you are in a business meeting or going to an upscale restaurant. Foreign business people tend to want to deal with someone who looks successful.

Malaysian-based YinLi Chua has a philosophy that helps her to make sure any international business guests feel right at home. Chua says that she has been dealing with international visitors for more than ten years and has conducted many successful international business deals. She says: "The main thing is I never put my energy and concentration into worrying that things won't go well. I treat all visitors as my good friends. I ask what they like, what they want to do. This simple care will give you all the answers you need to know about their culture, styles, and etiquette."

Chua emphasizes the benefits of being confident when you entertain your international business guests and in making them feel welcome: "When you're relaxed and happy, your visitors can feel relaxed and happy, too. That usually means the deal is done happily as well."

CHAPTER 6

# Tips on International Business Travel

If you are already a veteran international traveler you can probably skip this chapter. But, if you are a newcomer to the global marketplace, sooner or later, you are likely going to travel to another country for business. Whether it is for a few days to a trade show, a week to a distant location, or a couple of months to work on a project as a consultant for a multinational company, here are tips to help make that trip a pleasant one.

If you have an in-person meeting planned in a country you have never traveled to before or, if you traveled there more than three or four years ago, do some research about what you should wear to the meeting. In addition to dress, you will want to learn about a particular country's language, value system, and main religions, especially as these things pertain to the persons with whom you are meeting. Also find out about any safety and security issues, as well as any unique business practices or styles of greeting in the places you are visiting.

If you are traveling to a new country for a conference or trade show for meetings with a diverse number of fellow attendees from many countries around the world, you will want to learn as much as possible about the various cultures of the individuals you will be meeting with. You will also want to know what to expect in the city or country where the trade show is taking place.

## TIMING YOUR TRIP

Obviously if you work for a multinational corporation and your boss says, "I want you in our Beijing office in two months," you will have little input about what might be the ideal time for your business trip. But if you have control over when you take your trip, you can factor in some of these concerns:

- How much time do you need to prepare for your trip so you know enough about the protocol of the country you are visiting? Will you have time to do due diligence on the individuals with whom you will be meeting, as well as their companies or industry?

- Weather—Is there an ideal time when the weather is pleasant, not too hot or cold, and less of a chance of hurricanes, tsunamis, or monsoons?

- Holidays or vacation days—Can you plan the trip so it will not conflict with official holidays or vacation time? Or can you plan a trip that is long enough so you can use those holidays to travel on your own?

- Based on your host company's work load as well as your own, is there an optimum time for this trip?

- Can you build into your trip some "down time?" As Monica Marcel of Language and Culture Worldwide, Inc., notes, "If you're trying to get a business deal or develop a new relationship, try not to appear rushed. Try to build-in a couple of extra days to your trip. The first time I went to Rio, my business contact there invited me to their family island. She would never have thought to do that in advance. But once I was there, she asked me. The fact that I was able to do that won me points. Now we have a great business relationship." Having time in your schedule can allow for your host to make a connection with you that might not happen if you are rushing from arrival to meetings to immediately returning home.

## PREPARING FOR THE TRIP

Getting ready for your first international business trip is a defining moment for anyone doing business globally, whatever your age. That first trip is going to be the one that leaves the strongest impression on you. Your employer or the clients or customers with whom you meet do not know or care if it is your first trip or your tenth. You want to make a positive impression and have as successful an experience as possible.

There are some things that each international business traveler has to learn "first hand." Not every potential concern can be addressed in advance, especially in just one chapter in a book. But there are still enough universal issues that you can plan for in advance that should help you to do better during your first or subsequent international business trips. Even if you cannot control everything, advance planning could still make some disasters somewhat less likely. For example, although no one can control the weather, if you have any flexibility around dates for your global trip, try to pick times when the weather is optimum and hurricanes or tsunamis are the least likely to occur.

## TRY TO GET A LOCAL HOST TO MAKE ARRANGEMENTS FOR YOU

Try to arrange to have a local host make arrangements for you. This is not only useful because you will probably not know what hotel is closest to the company where you'll be attending meetings, or where to find the safest neighborhoods, but it also helps your local host to have a connection to you before you arrive, even if you have never met. Furthermore, if something unexpected happens, someone local then knows where you are and can help out with sharing that information.

World traveler Monica Marcel, a former Peace Corps volunteer and now an international consultant, says her business partner was recently in Mexico for a training session when there was a murder in his building, so he promptly moved to another hotel. Because he had made his own arrangements, the company that he was working with didn't know where he was. This could have been a real problem, but he was fluent in Spanish and able to get word to the company about his new location. When you are on an international business trip, remember to keep whatever business connections or businesses you are dealing with informed about where you are staying or how to contact you.

## PASSPORT AND VISAS

Because of the increased demand by more countries for passports, the U.S. government is advising citizens to allow four to six weeks for processing the required paperwork. Expedited service is possible, for a higher fee—$60 plus regular charges and overnight delivery charges—but even that is taking much longer now than just a few years ago. (Expedited service is currently two to three weeks.)

Whether or not you are required to get a visa for international travel will depend on the country you are planning to visit as well as the country you are from. In addition to the time it takes to get a passport, make sure you check with the country where you are traveling to find out if a visa is required. Even if it is possible to apply for a visa online, there may be a delay of one or more days from when your application is filed, to the issuing of the visa. Make sure you budget for those delays in planning your trip.

## VACCINATIONS AND MEDICATIONS

Some countries require vaccinations. (You can find much of this information online.) Or you can also ask your local host or liaison for guidance about this. Or ask colleagues or friends who have recently been to that region, for their suggestions.

If you are planning a business trip to Vietnam, for example, at www.guidevietnam.com you will find that they recommend consulting your doctor on what vaccinations you need and to bring along a small first-aid kit. The following vaccines are recommended for Vietnam: polio, tetanus, yellow fever, typhoid, and Japanese encephalitis. Your personal first aid kit should have drugs that deal with stomachaches and headaches.

If you take regular medications that may be difficult to replace while you are traveling, pack enough for your trip as well as an extra supply. Make sure you pack your medications in a place that is accessible to you at all times; avoid putting your only set of medications in your suitcase in case it is lost or delayed. You should also bring along an extra set of prescriptions from your physician in case you lose your medications; you could at least have the opportunity to replace them locally, especially if you take daily medications, since trying to get medications over-nighted from one country to another can take anywhere from two to four days.

## BUSINESS CARDS

If you have a business card that you use every day, you may want to amend it for your global business trip. For example, you may want to add "USA" to your card. If you are traveling to a trade show where you will be meeting people from all over the world, it might be advantageous to put it on your card, as part of your address, especially if you live in a little-known town. You also might want to spell out the name of the state you work in, such as "Florida" rather than "FL" since those you meet from outside the U.S. do not always know what the abbreviations stand for.

Make sure you include as high a title as appropriate since this will also increase the range of employees with whom you can meet. Some cultures also value degrees, such as an MBA, JD, or Ph.D.

As noted earlier, if you are traveling to Asia, have your business card in two languages, English on one side and the language of the country you are visiting on the other. This is a common practice for those working in Asia who are traveling internationally for business, but less common for Americans. It could, however, be very welcome when you are imprinting cards for your trip to show your consideration for those you are visiting by providing a dual language version of your business card. If you are wondering who in the United States might be able to print your cards in both languages, ask the business center at the hotel where you are staying on your trip to Asia. They might be able to arrange the printing for you and have it ready upon your arrival. Make sure you find out if there will be any surcharge beyond the printing charges so you can decide if it is reasonable, affordable, or not.

There is a growing trend to have only an e-mail or website address on a business card, especially for companies that are mainly Internet-based. If possible, try to also have a physical address. Not only does this indicate that you are more of a company than just a name or a vague Internet site but it helps those you meet internationally to see what region or country you are from. This can be a conversation starter and, if those you meet with want to follow up via land-mail, they are able to do so more easily.

Have enough business cards to give out during your international trip. If you are attending a trade show, you may find each person you meet wants two cards, one to have personally and one to put in their notebooks for possible follow-up. Running out of cards can be one of the more annoying and embarrassing aspects of an international business trip. It is not that easy to scramble to have more cards printed, even in the finest hotels, when you are traveling to distant lands. So have enough cards on hand with extras tucked away in your suitcase.

As noted earlier in this book, in some cultures, especially Asian ones, not only is what is written on a business card sacrosanct, but how the business card is handled is crucial. Once you are given a card, be careful what you do with it. I remember being told how one international traveler seriously harmed a business relationship by taking the business card he had just been given and folding it over and putting it in his back pocket. This was a sign of disrespect for that businessperson's card. Instead, the card should have been treated like a valuable and cherished object, read carefully and then thoughtfully placed into a business card holder.

## UNFORESEEN CHALLENGES

You can prepare as much as possible for that first international business trip but sometimes unforeseen challenges occur that can tax even the most seasoned traveler, let alone someone just starting out.

Monica Hemingway was a project director for a major telecommunications company when she was asked to go to Japan to give a talk at an annual customer conference for one of her firm's largest clients. She had never been to Japan before so she prepared by reading *Kiss, Bow, or Shake Hands* and also a book on business travel for women. She asked endless questions of everyone she knew who'd been to Japan. The big issue was gifts—what to bring for her hosts and what she could and could not accept from them. The night before her flight, she played in a hockey game and ended up getting hurt. She arrived in Japan in a wheelchair. Says Hemingway:

The rest of the trip was awkward but a good learning experience. Language barriers—giving a presentation with simultaneous translation and then answering audience questions through a translator—was a surreal experience. Strange eating habits and food, such as raw chicken and beef tongue, were delicious but unexpected. Having a live fish chopped to pieces in front of me and then being presented with the head was a little more disconcerting.

Misunderstanding gestures, such as flapping your hand at someone means 'come here,' not 'hello.' One night I drank way too much *sake* and to this day I still can't face the stuff. I spent an afternoon at a *kabuki* show. It went on for a long time.

It's one thing to read or hear about a country, its people, and its customs, it's quite another to actually be there. I thought I was fairly well prepared before I went. As it turns out, nothing would've prepared me for the five days I spent there. But being flexible, open to new experiences, being non-judgmental, and friendly went a long way in making it a positive experience rather than a disaster.

Rachna Kumar, Ph.D., Program Director of Business and Management Programs at Alliant International University in San Diego, California and an international business consultant, was in Dubai with another woman for a business project and company launch. But she and her colleague were never allowed to take charge of any of the meetings even though they outranked the men. She regretted not asking a male colleague to accompany her. She agrees that more preparation in recognizing the gender disparities in business culture in Dubai could have made her business there more successful. As she explains: "It was hard to control the flow of the agenda in a meeting in Dubai compared to meetings in any other country I've worked at. In my experience, in Dubai, you will not be taken seriously as a woman. The flow of the meeting was not in our hands." Next time Dr. Kumar would make sure she was part of a two-person team which included a woman and a man.

A 57-year-old Greek publisher based in Athens shared with me something about her country that she wishes those doing business with her would realize. She says, "Greeks are actually hard working but actually getting something done in Greece is difficult so other people consider Greeks lazy or laid back."

## SAFETY AND SECURITY

Business men and women traveling alone need to be aware of safety and security issues in the countries they plan to visit. This is especially true for women traveling alone. Barbara Farfan, an Orlando, Florida-based consultant's first international business trip was to the island of Bali on October 12, 2002. She arrived just hours before a terrorist attack left 202 people dead. The attack occurred less than five miles from her hotel. At the time, she worked for a powerful international corporation so she was able to get a flight out of the country as soon as those arrangements could be made. But she realized if she had been a consultant or self-employed, it might have been a lot harder to get priority treatment. What Farfan learned from that experience has helped her to better prepare for future international business trips.

She recommends anyone traveling internationally to "get the address and phone number of the U.S. Embassy and have it with you in several secure places before you step on the plane. Most governments and even transportation companies will give priority to taking care of their own citizens first in a time of crisis." In that way, if evacuations become necessary because of safety, health, or weather emergencies, you can quickly contact them for help. You might also want to consider registering with the U.S. Embassy, letting them know that you are visiting for business. The Embassy may be advised of political or other situations requiring evacuation before the public at large; but they can notify you only if you have registered with them.

Monica Marcel is a partner at the Chicago-based Language & Culture Worldwide, LLC, which does international training around the world. Monica has been robbed in six different countries including Brazil, Romania, Latvia, Russia, India, and the United States. Although each time had its own set of circumstances, there were some common denominators to the experiences that others might find useful:

1. If possible, avoid using a backpack when traveling internationally. When Monica was in Russia, she was walking in the market and the robber used a razor blade to cut the bottom of the backpack.

2. If you are taking a train, especially if you are going to sleep on it, as Monica did on one of her trips to India, make sure everything is under your feet or under your body. "I had just a bag that was in the seat next to me while I was napping. Someone swiped it. Luckily my wallet was strapped on to me" so it and her passport were not taken.

3. If you have hosts that you trust in the country you are visiting, listen to their advice. Monica might have avoided being robbed in Brazil if she had paid more attention to what her hosts cautioned about not going on a particular beach at dusk.

## PACKING

With airlines restricting the weight, size, and number of suitcases today without imposing hefty fines on the traveler it is much more likely that you will pack wisely than ever before. But you still have to be careful about just how much you plan to bring since you may be required to personally get your suitcase up and down stairs or even in and out of taxis or public transportation on a continual basis throughout your trip.

I traveled to Japan a few years ago to conduct several workshops. I wanted to bring as many materials in my suitcase as possible, as well as changes of clothes, so I would not have to ship things over in advance. I filled up the biggest suitcase I owned and I managed to get everything into that one bag. The problem was that it was so heavy I quickly got exhausted from pushing the suitcase around. It definitely had a negative impact on my trip.

For future trips, I took a suitcase that was almost half the size and shipped materials in advance to the hotel where I was staying so I was not as hampered by heavy papers, materials, or an oversized suitcase.

It might seem obvious but it definitely bears repeating: pack as lightly as possible and pack a few days in advance so you can check and double-check that you have everything you need for your business meetings. You can wear the same clothes twice, as long as the clothes are still clean, but not if you are meeting with the same people. If you want to pack as lightly as possible, have an assortment of blouses or shirts and ties to alter the look of a basic business suit. Most hotels provide irons to get rid of the wrinkles.

## WHAT TO WEAR

In most regions of the world, a business suit or business casual for most tech companies will be perfectly acceptable in any business meeting or setting. But in some cultures, you may have to adopt the native dress if you are to be allowed in meetings, especially if you are a woman business traveler who wants to meet with a man. Once again, it is best to find out the protocol in advance; ask what is expected of you so you can wear the appropriate clothes and bring along additional outfits that also will be acceptable. If this is your first trip to a region, or your last trip was in the distant past, find out what the current expectations are.

If you're traveling to Italy for business, for example, as Peter Farina, President of ItalyMONDO! LLC points out, "The Italians are very fashion conscious." As Farina, who works out of an office in Italy, says "I actually learned firsthand during my business trips to Italy that 'dress to impress' isn't just a recommendation but a necessity when conducting business in Italy. An Italian businessperson will always make their first impression based on how one dresses. It is a sign of success. One could show up with all the knowledge, money, credentials, and ideas needed but still lose the deal if their shoes were unshined or their jacket wrinkled. You could have all the credentials in the world, but you would not even get your foot in the door without looking the part."

Sometimes you have to improvise if your suitcase doesn't arrive at your destination. That is what happened to Thomasina Tafur, who worked for an international shipping corporation for twenty years. When the company opened its first office in India, she went there with a colleague to teach a class to a new sales force. Tafur explains: "My friend and I decided to go a few days early and see the sights. When we arrived in Delhi, our luggage was nowhere to be found. The airline gave us each $100 to buy new clothes at 'the mall.' It turns out what they call a 'mall' is really a market. So with our money, we bought four *saris* each. We decided to make the best of it and not let it ruin the entire trip. We loved the clothes so much—they're very comfortable—we wore them for most of the trip." Their luggage arrived four days later.

Barbara DesChamps has studied dress around the world and is author of two books in her *It's in the Bag* series, on the subjects of lightweight travel and business travel wardrobes. She shared an anecdote about a television announcer in Hong Kong who found herself in an embarrassing situation because she was wearing a red suit, which is considered an auspicious color in China. There had been a natural disaster and she had to go on camera to report the disaster without having time to change her clothes. Unfortunately she was in this bright red suit giving condolences.

To avoid finding yourself in a similar situation, DesChamps recommends that you always have a dark suit on your business trip, navy blue or black, just in case you have to deal with a somber occasion. You can then dress it up or dress it down with accessories.

## *While on Your Trip*

### GREETINGS

Good first impressions are vital in developing international business relationships which makes knowing how to offer a proper greeting extremely important.

Rahul Mehendale, a 35-year-old New Jersey-based entrepreneur, travels extensively to Germany, Serbia, and India for his business, myskin.com. Mehendale has figured out that he can get along in any international business meeting, whether or not he knows the native language, as long as he is able to say four things: "Hello" and "Goodbye"; "Thank You"; and "This is great." He either searches the Internet or asks a friend how to say those phrases before he leaves on every trip. As Mehendale explains, "What I realized from a negotiation perspective is if you can start by saying 'hello' in a local language, the comfort level just goes up exponentially."

Mehendale learned this lesson when he was a system engineer for one of the top independent diesel engine manufacturing companies headquartered in the Midwest. He had to give a presentation to several visiting Japanese executives. He decided he would learn the opening to his presentation in Japanese. His boss tried to discourage him from speaking in Japanese. He said that it usually backfired. But Mehendale had practiced and he was convinced it would be an asset. He began by saying, in Japanese, what his name was and what an honor it was to have the Japanese executives there. He continued the presentation in English.

That night, when the five Japanese executives went out to dinner with the executive team from the manufacturing company—two presidents and one vice president—they personally requested that Mehendale join them. "They asked for me to be there," he says with obvious pride.

Peter Farina, President, ItalyMONDO! LLC, whose office is in Italy, says there are distinct greetings that are expected if you are doing business in Italy. "One doesn't enter an office or home without saying *permesso*—as in, 'permission to enter,'" he says. "Also, one doesn't begin eating until everyone at the table is served and someone says *buon appetito*. And one doesn't leave a group or conversation early without saying *permesso*—permission. Greetings are never *ciao* in the beginning or in first meetings but *Buon Giorno* (morning to after lunch), *Buona Sera* (after lunch, into the evening) and *Buona Notte* (the last goodbye before going to bed). *Arriverderci*, and the formal *Arriverderla*, are the standard 'goodbye' regardless of time of day."

## LANGUAGE

English is spoken in hotels that cater to Westerners in most major cities around the world. In many countries English is the second language everyone learns which means it generally will be possible to communicate and be understood at least when it comes to your basic needs. If you are traveling for business and English is not the first language for your business associate, consider hiring an interpreter for your trip, especially if you will be doing any business negotiations.

Even if you flatter your business associates by saying a couple of things in their language, the nuances and subtleties of each language are just too important to risk derailing a business negotiation or contract because of an unwitting misunderstanding or misinterpretation. As Jan Diggs, an American working in Cairo for the last four years, points out, hiring someone to travel with you who is fully bilingual is definitely a consideration for business purposes. She explains: "I speak a little Arabic and understand a good bit more, so there are lots of cases in which I think I understand and then find that I've missed something important in the context. I always work and travel with someone who knows the language fully so that I can make sure I have all the information I need to do my job."

Diane DiResta, an international speaker and author of *Knockout Presentations*, did a management training seminar for the London office of one of the major U.S. financial services corporations. She thought it would be easy because there was no language barrier, or so she believed. During one of the training modules, she happened to reference packing her luggage and mentioned that she brought a pair of black pants. Suddenly, she heard snickering in the room. It turned out that "pants" are not slacks but underwear. From then on, she was more careful. Then she said "These are skills you can use back on the job." Suddenly, the entire room broke out in laughter. She quickly learned that "on the job" in England referred to a prostitute turning a trick.

## GESTURES

Familiarize yourself with the typical gestures that are used in the country you are visiting, such as kissing from cheek to cheek in certain Mediterranean countries. As Peter Farina of ItalyMONDO! LLC points out, in Italy, remember that you kiss from the right to the left. As Farina notes, "Many gaffes have been made where you get confused about which side to begin and end up planting one right in the middle!"

Gestures are definitely cultural phenomena that need to be studied and understood, based on whatever region you're traveling to. For example, as international business consultant Michael Soon Lee points out, "In Asia, when people nod, it doesn't necessarily mean they agree, just that they are listening."

## Getting Around

Even if every businessperson you meet with in other countries speaks English, you may find that taxi drivers, especially in the smaller cities, often do not. That's why it is important to write down your destination's address so you can show it to the driver. Many taxis today are equipped with GPS systems, or the driver has a cell phone that has a GPS system in it.

In India, there are drivers who pull people around on rickshaws attached to a bicycle. You have to be careful about how much you tip. When I first visited India, I was about to give a rickshaw driver a $1 tip for a $1 ride which, in those days, was considered extravagant. The businessman I was meeting with got very upset as he said, in an angry voice, "You Americans spoil them and ruin it for the rest of us." I have learned, however, that even though I thought my wish to tip the rickshaw driver a dollar was an acceptable gesture, it was out of line with what is expected in that country. Even today, a $1 tip would be considered extravagant in India. From Monica Marcel I learned that a more appropriate tip would be 10 or 20 rupees. If you are taking a taxi, however, you would tip on the basis of the size of the fare. "You might tip as much as 100 rupees, which would be around $2—especially if that driver has been with you for the whole day or if you will be using the same driver over multiple days," Monica says. She also told me when in Sweden, locals have let her know they considered it an insult to tip someone in Sweden. "In Sweden I was told, 'We have a social welfare system and we don't need you to throw your money around," says Monica. "In the United States, wait staff in restaurants are often paid less than minimum wage, and depend on the tips to earn enough to pay rent and eat."

## Where Will Business be Conducted?

In the United States, some business transactions occur on the golf course as often as they do over lunch in a restaurant. Find out what is expected in whatever country that you are traveling to.

Lindsay Adams is an international speaker based in Brisbane, Australia and former president of the Global Speakers Federation. He says that in

Singapore, if you are planning to meet someone for business, it will usually be conducted over a meal, be it breakfast, lunch, or dinner. Your host will always insist on paying and the more important a guest you are, the better quality food and venue will be chosen for you.

Every culture, and even each profession within a culture, will have its own rules and protocol for where to conduct a business meeting. So be careful about what offers you make unless you know the protocol regarding invitations and meals. You might just want to have your meeting in an office setting if that is considered appropriate to avoid any awkwardness about who would pick up the meeting meal tab if held in a restaurant.

## TRADE SHOWS

For many in the business world, attending an international trade show is often their first global business trip. Doing so presents different challenges than if you met with business men or women in their home offices. On a certain level, it's going to be an easier international business trip because everyone you meet will have the shared experience of attending the same trade show, usually in a location that is not

*The Internet is a great tool for advertising your products or services, but how do you attract potential buyers to your site? A good way to let people know about your offerings it to participate in international trade fairs or professional conferences in your industry or sector.*

the home office for a majority of the attendees. On another level, it will be harder because you will not be positioned as the business traveler who is hosted and maybe even wined and dined by your international business colleague in his or her city. Since you are meeting at the trade show, your cultural differences may actually be heightened when it is just the two of you sitting across a table from each other or at a trade show stand.

Although you are there to sell or buy products, or get new clients or customers, trade shows are still very much about relationship building. You want to give out your business card, but you also want to get the business cards of those you meet. It is recommended that you develop a system for writing down details about each person. This will help jog your memory upon your return, when you are going through the dozens of cards that you have collected, as well as when you are trying to deal with any follow-up requests. In fact, developing a system that works for you is a key part of making the trade show experience worth all the time, effort, and money that is entailed. If you do not have an efficient system for keeping track of who you meet, and, more importantly, what they have asked you to do to follow-up on your meeting, you might as well stay home!

Some write directly on the business cards. Others have a notebook and they even bring along a little stapler so they can staple each business card on a separate page, writing notes about the person and their meeting under the stapled card. (Be careful, however, if you plan to write on a business card or staple it in the presence of the card holder. Some cultures, particularly Asian, might be offended by treating a business card in that fashion.) Still others use their electronic organizers or a loose-leaf notebook system to keep track of each meeting and the follow-up that is ahead. Some, upon returning from the trade show, use a scanning device that will electronically add the business cards into their computer with speed and even quite a bit of accuracy.

When you sort through the cards of those you had met, it is useful to categorize them as either "hot" leads, or strong possibilities; "warm" leads, good for networking but not particularly timely; or "cool" leads, with nothing to rush to pursue. If you are doing the follow-up on your own, picking the right people to follow-up with is as crucial as following up in a timely manner. It's a race to the finish line, and the competition for the winning pay-off is fierce. Being first to get someone's attention after the trade show can make the difference between a sale or a pass. If possible, maintain contact (through e-mail) with someone back home who can be mailing out promotional material or samples before you even return from your trip.

> When you sort through the business cards of those you had met, it is useful to categorize them as either "hot" leads, or strong possibilities; "warm" leads, good for networking but not particularly timely; or "cool" leads, with nothing to rush to pursue. If you are doing the follow-up on your own, picking the right people to follow-up with is as crucial as following up in a timely manner.

Some people tack on a few days before or after the trade show for additional business visits at the offices of individuals whom they did not get to see at the trade show—or for sightseeing. Since you've come this far, why not take advantage of the opportunity, especially if it's in a once-in-a-lifetime location you might not get to visit again?

It's up to you if you want to go early for your sightseeing or visiting, rather than extending your trip after the show. There are pluses and minuses to each choice. If you go early, as Dan Poytner, an international speaker and author points out, you can get over your jet lag before your important meetings begin. The disadvantage is that you are taking away those days that you could have been using for last-minute revisions in the materials that you will be showing at the trade show as well as for necessitating that you reconfirm your appointments much further in advance than if you had not chosen to be gone before the trade show. The disadvantage of extending your trip after the show is that what you do in the first couple of days or the week after the trade show can be pivotal to grabbing that new business or making sure your old business isn't wooed away by a competitor.

The best piece of advice I was ever given about how to make a trade show more effective as a relationship and business builder was shared with me by Ib Lauritzen, a literary agent in his 80s who is based in Denmark and who has attended or exhibited at every Frankfurt Book Fair since the fair started more than fifty years ago. Ib said to me, "You have fifty-one other weeks during the year to sell books." What he meant was that for him, the Frankfurt Book Fair is about meeting people, and making connections, not doing the "hard sell" that so many others considered it to be. When Ib and his wife and business partner, Bebbe, and I meet at the Frankfurt Book Fair, if possible, it is for breakfast or lunch, rather than a rushed half-hour appointment. (My favorite meeting with Ib and Bebbe, however, was when I went to Denmark and Sweden for business and I had a "courtesy call" with them; I was treated to a Scandinavian smorgasbord that they graciously prepared for me and my family in their home in a town outside of Copenhagen.)

## MEETING AND SEATING PROTOCOL
## AND BUSINESS MEETINGS

Be mindful of what the meeting and seating protocol is in each country that you visit. For example, as noted in Chapter 1, when Min Chan went to China, she went to a dinner function with her mother. "I sat down first," she says, thinking back on her etiquette breach with embarrassment. "Next time, I made sure that I waited until everyone arrived before sitting down at the banquet table, another sign of respect."

In some cultures, like Japan, it could be a long time before you even get to your business meeting. According to author Michael Soon Lee, he spent two weeks in Japan just touring, singing karaoke, and drinking *sake* before he ever got down to business with the people he was meeting with. He said they wanted to first determine whether or not he was a "good person." If he had ever brought up the subject of business, the deal would have instantly died.

Where business entertaining occurs is very much a cultural matter. For example, New Zealanders prefer to entertain in their homes for business. However, because homes and apartments in Poland may be on the smaller size, you are more likely to find yourself being entertained in a restaurant. You are also likely to be entertained at a restaurant for a business dinner in Sweden. And when you out to a restaurant for a business dinner in Spain it will probably start a lot later at night, beginning as late as 9 p.m.

### FOOD

Practically everyone has a food story when they travel internationally. I recently had an experience on a business trip to Madrid, Spain that involved a *faux pas* around food. I was looking over the menu, in Spanish, as my two business colleagues asked what I'd like to eat. Unfortunately, everything I kept asking about turned out to be Mexican food, not Spanish. I ended up ordering what they were having, a gazpacho soup with ham in it, which turned out to be a pink color and very distinctive from the red gazpacho I was used to, but I ate it politely.

When entrepreneur Daniel Avery started doing business in China eight years ago, he went out to dinner with his Chinese counterparts who had brought him to a semi-resort for dinner. When walking up to the main building, he noticed a small, glassed-in structure to his right, filled with cages housing a variety of animals. A dog and a peacock both grabbed his attention and he remembers saying out loud, "Wow, they have a petting zoo for the children!" Needless to say, he was naive back then. Long story short: the peacock was served at dinner that night. He did eat a bit of it—later describing it as terribly perfume-y. He supposes that since he appeared to be interested in the bird, they thought he wanted to eat it.

Jan Diggs is General Manager of Business Development for Arabia Inform, a media intelligence and content company based in Cairo, with offices in Dubai and Washington, D.C. She went to a conference in Riyadh, Saudi Arabia where the hosts tried to honor her by serving her buffet plate with a whole roasted sheep's head, which is considered the prime part of the animal. Fortunately the people who offered the sheep's head were aides from the host organization so she was able to say "no thank you" and not cause offense or an international incident. Had it been their bosses, she says she "would have taken it and found some way to eat a bite or two without getting sick."

## MEANWHILE, BACK HOME...

There is that old cliché, "out of sight, out of mind," and that holds true for the international business traveler. You do not want your boss, colleagues, or employees forgetting you while you're away.

How can an employee who will be gone for months or years on an assignment in another country protect his or her seniority back home? One fear is that they will be passed over for advancements because they are not in the home office. On the other hand, in some companies, being sent to work internationally is seen as a training ground for getting a promotion upon return as well as having something very impressive to add to one's resume because of the global experience. But making sure there is a job to come back to is still something that needs to be considered.

Here are some ways to make sure those left behind at work do not forget you while you're traveling or temporarily relocating internationally:

- Use a Blackberry or a similar device that gets e-mails instantly around the world, such as an Apple iPhone or iPad, and stay up on as many communications as possible as if you're still right there in the home office.

- If your department has a regular team meeting, figure out the time difference and ask to be included via calling in or using a pass code. Even if you need to bring a pre-paid calling card, use a free service like Skype.com, or just have a mobile phone that works internationally, call those who are important to you and your job regularly. Do not just rely on e-mail because it's more convenient and free. Communicating by phone will go far in keeping you in the loop and helping everyone who counts, such as your boss, key colleagues, or employees, to remember you however your long your business trip turns out to be.

## *After the Trip*

### RECONNECTING AT THE OFFICE

It's hard when you're away and trying to travel light to think about bringing souvenirs back for each and every coworker. But if you can possibly manage it, you will reap the rewards. Remember, it is usually harder to be the one left behind than the one who goes on the trip, especially an exciting international one. Traveling globally for business is very hard work but to those who are back in the office facing the day-to-day routine, it seems glamorous and exciting. By picking up some inexpensive mementos of your trip, you will be showing that you were thinking of your colleagues and you will also be sharing a bit of that foreign culture with them. Try to pick something that will be useful, or that is unique to that culture, or that would be fun to have even though there's no intrinsic value to it. Food gifts are another favorite but avoid buying something that is readily available at home since that will diminish the uniqueness of your gift.

How you handle your international business trip with your peers can be very challenging since you do not want to boast or brag. But if you focus too heavily on the sacrifices and difficulties of the trip, you will find little sympathy in the eyes of those who did not get to go.

## FOLLOW-UP

It is so easy to get caught up in all the work that has accumulated while you were away. However, remember your manners and send an e-mail, a card, a token present, or call and thank everyone who met with you and went out of their way to help you to feel at home in their city or country. If you promised to follow-up on anything that was discussed at your meetings, let the appropriate people know that you are either sending that information immediately or that you need more time and will have it ready by a specific date.

To reiterate: international business trips can help strengthen a developing relationship, but all the time, energy, and monetary investment in your trip could be wasted if you fail to take the time to thank those who helped you along your way.

CHAPTER 7

# *Gift-Giving, Legal Considerations, and Ethics[1]*

In the enthusiasm of going global, it is sometimes easy to overlook the fact that certain rules for doing business internationally can be different than those which govern similar transactions in the United States, especially when it comes to gift-giving or legal and regulatory matters. Each country's legal system is distinctive; contracts have different values in other cultures, and business practices can be challenging for a first-time exporter or contractor. Understanding these distinctions can make the difference between a nice profit and a steep loss or worse. This chapter focuses on those rules—or lack thereof—as well as how to address corruption and potentially unethical practices in other countries so you can conduct your business safely and efficiently while still complying with U.S. laws.

## GUIDELINES FOR GIFT-GIVING

The range of acceptability regarding the exchange of gifts with on-going or potential international business partners varies from country to country. To make things even more confusing, the rules that govern this also change from time to time. So, the best strategy regarding gifts is to ask someone in the international office where you are visiting, or a colleague who has been there recently. Should you bring a gift, or not? And if a gift is expected or appreciated, how much should you spend on it? Be careful to have whoever answers your questions define what is meant by "gift." For example, in *Kiss, Bow, or Shake Hands*, in the section on gift-giving customs in Kuwait, it is pointed out that "you are not required to bring a gift when invited to a Kuwaiti home." But in the very next sentence, you learn: "However, flowers or candy will be appreciated." Without that additional sentence, you might have shown up to your host's place empty-handed, believing that the definition of "gift" included flowers or candy.

---

[1] This chapter is not a substitute for professional legal advice. It is for very general information only. Please consult an attorney for any specific legal questions or concerns that you have.

In general, there's nothing wrong with bringing a token gift from your state or country for your international business associates. In fact, arriving with something for your host or hostess will likely go a long way in building a positive reputation for you. But you need to be aware of any guidelines that each company and country have about what is considered appropriate and acceptable in terms of how much you should spend on a gift, and what could be misconstrued as an attempt at influence peddling or bribery. If you do decide to give a gift in a business situation, offering something from your particular state or country could be well-received. However, be careful that whatever gift you are giving is from that actual location, such as maple syrup from Vermont, or a small replica of the Statue of Liberty that is actually from the state of New York and not stamped "Made in" another country. On the other hand, a piece of jewelry costing $100 or more could cause problems.

At this writing, $25 is the maximum allowed for a tax-deduction for business gifts in the United States, but you do not even have to spend that much to be polite and considerate. Flowers or candy are appreciated around the world. Just make sure you ask what type of flowers are acceptable and also how to present your gift.

Jeanette S. Martin and Lillian H. Chanery point out in *Global Business Etiquette* that you should avoid giving someone in Saudi Arabia or China a key chain with an eagle, the U.S. national bird, because in those countries an eagle signifies "bad luck." Whether or not the gift is opened in front of others also varies from country to country. Martin and Chanery point out that in Japan, Taiwan, Hong Kong, and South Korea, you do not open the gift in front of the gift-giver. Conversely, gifts are opened in front of the giver in Middle East countries, "to show that it is not a bribe."

As for flowers, there are a number of considerations about color and type in various cultures. Again, according to Martin and Chanery, follow these guidelines:

- Avoid roses (usually only for romantic partners).

- In China, do not give white flowers (the color of mourning).

- In Brazil, the lower class associates purple flowers with death.

- Avoid carnations in France and Germany, and chrysanthemums in Belgium, Japan, and Italy because those flowers are used to adorn cemeteries.

In her book *Put Your Best Foot Forward: Mexico/Canada*, Mary Murray Bosrock has this useful tip: bring a wrapped gift with you just in case you are given a gift. That way you will not be caught off guard without the ability to reciprocate a gift in return.

Wrap the gift before presenting it to your host or the company with whom you are visiting. Giving an unwrapped present makes it look like you did not take the time to plan, or that you were rushing and picked something up at the airport or along the way to your meeting. Be careful in your choice of wrapping paper, however, since certain colors might be offensive in some cultures, such as black and white paper in Japan.

Min Chan, a lawyer, says her former boss unwittingly brought unpopular gifts to China. Instead of bringing designer goods such as shirts, which would have been welcome, her boss bought obscure pins from a museum store. Chan says that bringing desirable gifts may lead to better outcomes in negotiations as it shows responsiveness. She points out that her supervisor disregarded her advice and the outcome was disappointing. "The negotiation went less than desirable," says Chan.

Chan was taught by her mother, who has a real estate business in China, that the best way to know what kind of gift you should bring on a business trip is to go about it as you would if looking for a local hotel or restaurant recommendation: ask someone you are working with internationally for suggestions. Chan says she will ask the staff in China about what is a popular gift, or what kind of gift do people want from the U.S. now? Over the years, Chan has brought various popular gifts to China that were well-received; her most recent offering was one of the top brands of chocolate, which at the time of her trip was hard to obtain in China.

In business, it is crucial to know whether gift-giving is expected or if it could be misconstrued as an attempt at influence peddling or bribery. Gift-giving etiquette in international business can range from Japan, where it is a strong expectation, to the United States, where it is much less common. It bears repeating that since gift-giving varies greatly country by country, it is imperative that you find out what is expected. It is also important to know what situations could sabotage your gift-giving. For example, *International Business Culture* author Charles Mitchell shares a very telling example of when General Motors Corporation was competing with other major manufacturers to secure a car manufacturing partnership with Shanghai Automotive Industrial. According to Mitchell, General Motors gave the executives gifts from Tiffany's jewelry store, being careful to replace the store's signature white ribbon with a red one because red is symbolic of luck in China, while white is associated with death or sadness.

In *Kiss, Bow, or Shake Hands*, co-authors Terri Morrison, Wayne A. Conaway, and George A. Borden point out that in Indonesia and China, do not give clocks, straw sandals or handkerchiefs as gifts; or gifts or wrapping paper where the predominant color is white, black, or blue because they are all associated with funerals. They also recommend avoiding any gifts of knives, cutting tools or scissors to the Chinese since any of those items "suggest the severing of a friendship."

As long as accepting a token gift is not an ethical breach, always be careful to be gracious and to say "thank you" even if the gift is something that you may not have a use for, or if you are offered food, like chocolates, that you might not eat because of dietary concerns.

In some cases you should send a "thank you" note or card, but not all. Nadja Specht of Nuvota Marketing says that sending a thank you note would be very unusual in Germany and considered an odd thing to do. But in other cultures, especially in the United States, sending a thank you note is considered to be polite and a way to strengthen a business relationship.

Once again, the key is for you to get to know what is expected of you in whatever culture or country you are focused upon, whether visiting yourself or hosting a business traveler. But you also want to be true to what is comfortable for you and your personality. Some people are okay with giving and accepting token gifts; for others, it makes them uncomfortable and confused. Some may wonder if there is there a hidden motive to the gift. Others agonize over what to buy or ask themselves how they should react when they open a gift, or even whether they are allowed to open it in front of their host. Also, you need to consider the relationship that you have with the person with whom you are giving the gift. You do not want to feel like a phony giving a gift just because it is expected, when you do not feel that kind of positive emotion toward someone.

## WHEN DOES A GIFT BECOME A BRIBE?

It was mentioned that in the United States there is a $25 ceiling on tax-deductible business gifts. The acceptable maximum for a business gift may vary from culture to culture but Americans have to be most concerned with their own corporate, legal and ethical guidelines about gift giving and receiving—including items such as expensive tickets to sport events—to avoid being put in a potentially compromising position that could lead to being accused of taking a bribe.

Some cultures may allow bribery as a way to motivate parties to want to do business with each other. But it is still against the law in the United States to either offer or accept a bribe whether you are on home soil or in another country. If you are steadfast about what is acceptable for you, you will not have to ponder whether you can, or cannot accept expensive gifts that may cross the line into bribery.

There's an interesting article by *Korean Times* columnist Jon Huer entitled, "Gift-giving and Bribery Culture in Korea," that highlights how difficult it can be in Korea to have a clear line between gift-giving and bribery. Huer extols the system in America of "going Dutch" whereby the bill for a business lunch or dinner is split among the diners, unless other arrangements were made, avoiding the issue of anyone being beholden to another. He contrasts that with the Korean culture whereby "most Koreans, being so infinitely conscious of their duty to others, practically fight for the honor of paying the whole bill for everybody. Sometimes, foreigners are astounded to witness a physical shoving match, as members push one another aside to rush to the counter to pay the bill."

Such largesse, however, can sometimes lead to complications. Huer writes, "the Korean gift-giving custom is wonderful as a cultural trait, but also troublesome if it involves government officials, as the line between gift and bribery tends to blur."

Similar concerns are expressed in an article in *The Times of India* which asked: "Can gifts become bribes?" The head of sales for a major Indian hotel goes on to explain why the silk ties, scarves, personalized daily diaries or plants are not considered bribes and that he gives "gifts only to strengthen relations, to say thank you for supporting us...We do not expect anything in return."

"Not expecting anything in return" is one major distinguishing factor between a gift and a bribe. There are other methods that help to dispel any notion of bribery such as food gifts that are sent to an individual but then shared with the rest of the staff.

> *"Not expecting anything in return" is one major distinguishing factor between a gift and a bribe. There are other methods that help to dispel any notion of bribery such as food gifts that are sent to an individual but then shared with the rest of the staff.*

But what should you do when you are dealing with a foreign culture with different standards and interpretations of what is acceptable than in your own country? You don't want to offend anyone, but at the same time you don't want to be accused of accepting a bribe.

Here's how one international business person handled an expensive gift. One of her overseas distributors gave her a Persian carpet at one of her firm's product launches abroad. Since it would have been considered an insult if she did not accept it, she took the rug and then regifted it to another distributor.

Someone else may have taken a different approach such as thanking the gift giver profusely for the generous gift but then return it, explaining that you have to decline such a lavish gift, or donate it to charity on their behalf. Just make sure you keep careful records of either the return of the gift or the donation.

Tennessee-based Thomasina Tafur worked for a major international shipping company for more than twenty years including extensive traveling around the world. She points out how she made it clear to her customers in Latin America that she was not allowed to participate in the bribery system that was "just a way of life in some parts of Latin America." Tafur says that her company "had very strict policies on what we could and could not give or receive. I was always clear with my customers, and after a while, they understood."

# FOREIGN CORRUPT PRACTICES ACT

While no one likes to pay bribes, it is especially important for Americans to be aware that U.S. law prohibits the practice of paying bribes or contributing to corruption. The Foreign Corrupt Practices Act (FCPA) makes it unlawful for a U.S. company or person to offer, pay or promise to pay money or give anything of value to any foreign official or foreign political party or candidate for the purpose of getting or retaining business. It is even unlawful to make a payment to any person while knowing that all or a portion of the payment will be given to a foreign official or political party or candidate in order to gain a favor from that person. It is similarly illegal for foreign persons or businesses to attempt to buy influence in the U.S.

Prohibited actions—including promises not meant to be kept—that involve corruption are:

- Influencing any act or decision of a foreign official in his or her official capacity.

- Inducing a foreign official to do or omit to do any act that violates his or her lawful duty.

- Inducing any foreign official to use influence with a foreign government or instrumentality to affect or influence any act or decision of such government or instrumentality.

- Securing any improper advantage.

"Foreign Official" is defined broadly to include officials at state-owned companies, politicians, military (former or active) and relatives of a ruling family member.

The FCPA also requires companies that have their equities listed on securities exchanges in the United States or filed with the Securities and Exchange Commission, including their foreign and domestic subsidiaries, and their officers, directors, employees and agents, to keep books, records, and accounts that fairly and accurately reflect the company's transactions and the disposition of its assets. These accounting and recordkeeping provisions apply equally to a company's domestic and foreign operations and reporting practices, and violations can occur regardless of whether a payment or offer to pay is made to a foreign official. In addition, the FCPA's accounting provisions apply to all payments, not just amounts that would be material in a business sense.

## CORRUPTION AND LEGAL SYSTEMS

One of the most difficult problems Americans face in going global is the widespread existence of official and locally acceptable corruption in many parts of the world. In some societies, it is a regular part of doing business for government officials and trading partners to demand bribes for everything from obtaining a license to import, to getting your goods through customs.

As reported in the *New York Times*, accounts of doing business or competing for contracts in Afghanistan have highlighted the prevalence of bribe-taking there: truck drivers complain that they cannot deliver their goods unless they pay bribes to police officers, while construction crews in the countryside must pay bribes to local government officials to gain building permits, and then pay additional bribes to others to be allowed to continue work on their buildings. Virtually all shipments that must clear customs, including fuel and supplies crossing the border to support international assistance and military operations, face the outstretched palms of officials demanding payments or they will hold up the trucks and vans crossing the border.

Afghanistan is not the only country where corruption is a fact of life. Transparency International, a respected non-governmental organization, keeps track of corruption around the world. It publishes an annual report called the Corruption Perception Index (CPI), which ranks countries according to the degree of corruption that a businessperson is likely to encounter there. The rankings go from #1, the least corrupt country to #170, the most corrupt. The 2009 Report lists Afghanistan as #169, or one of the most corrupt countries on the planet, exceeded only by Somalia. New Zealand ranks as #1, or the least corrupt country in the world, followed by Denmark. The United States comes in at #6. The CPI can be found at http://www.transparency.org. The website provides monthly news updates and offers advice on handling corruption.

## DIFFERENT LEGAL SYSTEMS

An equally challenging part of doing business internationally is making sense out of legal systems in other countries, and what your rights are in those countries. Elsewhere, rights which are protected in the United States, such as freedom of speech and assembly, freedom to worship and to distribute printed material are often restricted. Violating the host country's laws can lead to confiscation of your materials, arrest or expulsion from the country. According to a foreign service officer who spent twenty years "in the field" working internationally, this has happened to people who wanted to distribute Bibles or religious literature in China and Russia. Both of these countries restrict the rights of groups that are not officially registered and recognized to "proselytize"—which means that the importing, selling or distributing of religious texts may land you in jail. Similarly, importing pictures or texts considered offensive or containing sexually uninhibited content is considered an offense in many Muslim majority countries and carries a steep fine and possible criminal penalties.

Singapore is an example of a country that punishes, often harshly, violations of public decorum such as littering or spitting in the street. In 1994, an American teenager was sentenced to four months in jail, given a $1,400 fine, and received six lashes with a bamboo cane for vandalism, specifically spray-painting cars and throwing eggs. His sentence was eventually reduced to four lashes, after which he was expelled from the country.

Some foreign countries have a spotty record of enforcing court judgments and apply different rules to settling business disputes between citizens and foreigners. According to the retired foreign service officer, for example, in the Russian Federation, some American companies have complained that when they have taken their Russian counterparts to court and received a judgment against them, the judges had no ability to enforce the ruling. In one particular case, it meant the Russian company that was trying to take over the restaurant the American had opened in Moscow lost its legal case but kept the restaurant, forcing the American owner to leave the country empty-handed. In other cases in Russia, organized criminal groups have threatened and forced foreigners to abandon their property and leave the country or face violence and even death threats. There have been similar reports in countries ranging from Mexico to the Middle East, China and parts of Eastern Europe.

Although you cannot anticipate every possible problem when doing business internationally, it pays to do your homework and to learn about the laws and regulations of the country in which you want to invest or export. The U.S. Department of Commerce's Foreign Commercial Service publishes Country Commercial Guides for virtually every country with which the U.S. interacts. These list the main requirements for doing business in that country, including whether or not you need a license or registration to do business there, information about the legal system and special requirements for establishing bank accounts and taxes. These Codes can be found at http://www.export.gov and clicking on "Market Research" and going to the Country Commercial Guides section and then clicking on the country that you wish to research.

## INTELLECTUAL PROPERTY

Intellectual Property (IP) refers to the rights of authorship which are protected under copyright laws. This includes written words and music as well as inventions, designs, and trade secrets. Unfortunately, there is no international treaty which completely defines or protects this kind of property, and laws and regulations which protect such property differ widely from country to country.

*There is no universal treaty or agreement that protects fully your patent, trademark or copyright outside the country in which it is registered.*

National intellectual property laws spell out what the rights of owners are, and under what circumstances other people may have access to that property, but these laws only apply to that specific country's territory. U.S. patent, trademark registration, copyright or mask work (design of a semiconductor chip) registration extends only throughout the territory of the United States and its possessions and will not protect your intellectual

126

property in other countries. In fact, there is no universal treaty or agreement that protects fully your patent, trademark or copyright outside the country in which it is registered. To receive such protections, you have to research the laws in each country to which you intend to export your intellectual property and comply with the requirements established there.

That being said: a number of international treaties and conventions, as well as bilateral agreements between the United States and many other countries, have established minimum standards for the protection and enforcement of intellectual property rights. The U.S. is a party to the Berne Convention for the Protection of Literary and Artistic Works and the Universal Copyright Convention (UCC) which provide some measure of protection for artistic and literary works, music and software programs.

Under the Berne Convention, works created by a citizen of a Berne Union country, or works that are first or simultaneously published in a Berne Union member country, are automatically eligible for protection in every other Berne Union member country without registration or compliance with any other formality of law. This applies to works first published in the United States on or after March 1, 1989, the date on which the United States acceded to the Berne Convention. Works published before March 1, 1989 were protected in many countries under the UCC—if the works were published with the formalities specified in that Convention. Older works may also be protected as a consequence of simultaneous publication in a Berne country or because of bilateral agreements between the U.S. and another country. Since the regulations vary from one country to another, it is important to check the laws and the treaty obligations of any country where you intend to publish.

Despite the existence of some legal protections, one of the weak links of the international intellectual property system is enforcement. Some countries that have signed the Berne Convention or the Paris Convention or joined the WTO have a spotty record of enforcing trademark, copyright, and patent regulations. Anyone who has traveled to Southeast Asia has seen pirated videos, DVDs, knock-off designer handbags or luggage and other items for sale that are in violation of copyright, trademark or patent commitments made by the governments of countries in the region. This is also true in Russia and many parts of the former Soviet Union, the Middle East, and elsewhere.

To combat this flagrant piracy, the U.S. Government launched the Strategy Targeting Organized Piracy (STOP) in 2004. The initiative is designed to help small businesses secure and enforce their rights in overseas markets. It established a hotline that provides a "one-stop shop" for businesses wanting to protect their intellectual property at home and abroad. STOP also provides information to small businesses on how to reduce the risk of global piracy and counterfeiting, and how to protect intellectual property rights. Information about STOP can be found at www.stopfakes.gov.

The rampant theft of intellectual property including inventions as well as such goods as books and DVDs is another reason it may be helpful to you and your business or company to have a local partner or distributor for your products. It can be the best way to prevent or at least detect when abuses occur. This truth was brought home to me a few years back when I did an Internet search on my name and I found, to my surprise, a translation of one of my books in a language and territory that was completely news to me. I advised my agent in that country about what I had discovered and she immediately contacted the local publisher, who subsequently owned up to translating and publishing the book without permission or a contract. They agreed to sign a contract and pay a fee, retroactively. A similar situation occurred in another country within the last year. This time a businessman with whom I was negotiating a new business venture happened to discover an edition of one of my works that had not been authorized for publication. Once again, the publisher in violation of copyright was willing to pay a fee through a local agent. In the latter case, the guilty party was so worried about the potential consequences of being found out that he appeared at the agent's office, unannounced, and immediately paid to the agent the penalty fee for his intellectual property breach in cash.

## Getting Legal Advice

Before allowing your work to be exported or published abroad, you should consult a patent or copyright attorney. In fact, you should consider getting local legal advice before signing any contract or making a financial commitment or establishing a partnership or agency agreement in a foreign country.

There are two good sources for finding a reliable and trustworthy lawyer to help you with your business goals in a foreign country. First, consider checking with your U.S. lawyer or agent. Many large law firms have branch offices or affiliate relationships with lawyers in other countries who adhere to U.S. ethical and professional standards. Your lawyer in the U.S. can arrange an introduction or refer you to someone who will handle your professional and business dealings abroad.

A second good source is the U.S. Embassy or Consulate in a particular country. The U.S. Embassy's Consular Affairs American Citizens' Services office maintains lists of English-speaking lawyers who have assisted Americans in the past, have a positive professional track record, and are members of the local bar association, the Chamber of Commerce or other business professional organization. You can find the contact information for the U.S. Embassy or Consulate at http:www.state.gov and locating the country in which you are interested.

## Anti-Boycott Regulations

The U.S. has, as a matter of policy, opposed the practice of one country restricting trade or prohibiting imports or exports (boycotting) countries friendly to the United States. The policy was directed at certain Middle Eastern countries that made boycotting Israel a condition of doing business with them. The U.S., in turn, responded by requiring American companies or persons to reject the anti-Israeli boycott and to publicly report any attempt to get them to observe the boycott. My foreign service expert source shared with me that the policy is embodied in the provisions of the Export Administration Act and through a 1977 amendment to the Tax Reform Act of 1976. These laws prohibit U.S. exporters from participating

129

in foreign boycotts or taking actions to support such boycotts. Furthermore, U.S. companies who receive requests to comply with foreign boycotts must report them to the U.S. Department of Commerce and disclose publicly whether they have complied with such requests.

## ETHICS

To say that there is a consensus about business values would make things much simpler, but that is far from reality. Although the ideal is to be honest and forthright, in some cultures lying is considered a negotiating tactic. You will want to know what is allowed or standard in whatever culture you're doing business in, but that does not mean you have to agree to those behaviors. In my book *Business Protocol*, I devote an entire chapter to ethics: "Etiquette and Ethics: Is there a Connection?" It begins by defining etiquette and ethics: "Etiquette deals with what is considered *acceptable* by a society or within a given company; ethics is what is considered moral."

In conducting business internationally you are looking at ethics in a wide range of cultures and countries, rather than in a more homogeneous area, which only adds to the complexity of the question: is there a connection between etiquette and ethics?

Here are some business-related situations that could be considered a breach of ethics as well as etiquette:

- Exaggerating or lying about sales figures or profits. (Etiquette issue: it is polite to tell the truth; ethics issue: it is immoral and even illegal to misrepresent business information.)

- Posing as a potential customer or client to see what the competition is offering. (Etiquette issue: violation of trust and deception; ethics issue, misrepresentation.)

- Dragging out negotiations or payments. Etiquette issue: being prompt is considered correct business protocol. Ethics issue: unnecessary delays or lying about "the check is in the mail." This practice erodes confidence in an individual and a company and, as etiquette expert Camille Lavington says, "it makes you wonder if they are unethical about other business practices as well."

Here are other etiquette issues that are also examples of exemplary ethics:

- Keep your promises in business, especially about the delivery of goods or services. If there are extenuating circumstances that require you to get an extension, explain why it is necessary to ask for one.
- Be careful about criticizing employees or products, whether your own or your competitor's, especially in public.

An example of how ethics will trump etiquette was shared in an interview with Dorothea Johnson, who founded the Protocol School of Washington. As I noted in *Business Protocol*, Johnson was hired by a law firm to teach one of its up-and-coming lawyers better table manners. A few months after she trained him, she asked how he was doing. Johnson was surprised to find out that the young lawyer had been fired because he had been caught double-billing and the firm would not tolerate unethical behavior.

A refusal to tolerate unethical behavior is a useful guidepost for doing business internationally; but it can become complicated if another culture seems to find such behavior acceptable. Just because they may see nothing wrong with accepting a bribe or something similar, doesn't mean you have to deviate from your own ethical or legal values. Be clear about your standards and principles, and stick to them.

# CHAPTER 8

# *Negotiating*

Negotiating styles and steps differ from country to country. For example, when negotiating in many Middle Eastern countries it is considered very bad manners to get right to the point of the meeting and ask for what you want. Instead, there are social ceremonies, such as drinking tea and exchanging comments about the weather and other non-controversial topics (except not about women in the family). It is important to go into such a meeting with an understanding of what to expect. It may be a meeting just to start things going and to get to know each other and to set up a second meeting where more pertinent business topics will be discussed. The key is to be patient.

If the people you're negotiating with do not speak English you may need an interpreter. If so, make sure you know your interpreter well, and make available translations of any relevant materials. Using a go-between or advisor is also an effective strategy for these types of meetings. Remember that success must be measured in small steps.

Be firm but friendly; be polite, and be careful about trying to tell jokes. Humor doesn't always translate well and could be misconstrued or misunderstood. Always do your homework ahead of time to find out who has the leverage in the group with whom you are meeting. It may not always be the chief spokesman. Also, make sure you have invited the right people to the meeting. Much time has been wasted in meetings that failed to conclude deals because the person needed to approve the deal was not in attendance.

There are times when the meeting you are in may not even seem like a negotiation. Again, the best thing you can do is to be patient. Review any points that are made and agreed upon, and make successful meetings contingent on agreements to earlier steps. You also have to know when "yes" really means "yes" and when it means "maybe" or "no." This varies from country to country. Moreover, you need to clarify what you have been saying so that it is heard that same way by your negotiating partners.

Westerners see negotiations as a way to arrive at a "deal" while people in other cultures may view negotiations as a way to form a "relationship." It all depends on the culture. In such cases, it is important that both sides feel satisfied, especially if this is to be an on-going relationship. While many Westerners are very direct, they may have difficulty dealing with people who are indirect and who want to get to know you before actually negotiating terms.

> Westerners see negotiations as a way to arrive at a "deal" while people in other cultures may view negotiations as a way to form a "relationship." It all depends on the culture.

Negotiations have both formal and informal stages. In the informal stage, you are just gathering information about a product, person, or company that you might be doing business with especially if you will be buying or selling a product or service. The informal information gathering stage can be done over the phone in discussions, in searching out database with background statistics or details that might be useful to you when the formal stages of negotiations begin, as well as phone or in-person meetings at trade shows, seminars, or office visits whether across town, across the country, or on the other side of the globe.

The formal stages of negotiation in the U.S. include:

1.  Formal meetings with draft documents and information.
2.  Exchange of positions, offers and counteroffers.
3.  Caucuses (separate meeting) to discuss various issues.
4.  Subcommittees formed for specific topics.
5.  New proposals with explanations.
6.  Agreement, Signing, Implementation, or Impasse.
7.  If Impasse, perhaps request for a mediator or another forum or go to another party.

No matter what country you are doing business with, learn the negotiating stages in that particular country so you will know in advance what you might expect. A structured negotiation in China, for example, might follow this pattern:

1. General opening phase—pleasantries are exchanged.

2. Technical discussion—a long and drawn out but penetrating period.

3. Discussion over the terms of contract that might involve challenges on technicalities.

4. A contract signing proceeded by demands for new concessions.

5. The ongoing, post-contract negotiation.

In the opening phase, the Chinese Letter of Intent will aim high; it will outline the major provisions of the future contract agreement, and reflect the basis upon which the Chinese controlling authorities will permit the negotiating party to proceed to contract negotiations. These goals will have been determined by a committee and, once determined, the up-front negotiators will stick by these goals very strictly and strongly because to concede might mean losing face with their superiors.

Next is the Technical Discussion Phase. This can take months and stalling may help because the Chinese assume that Westerners are in a hurry. Time can be filled with tourist sights, banquets, and so forth, but it is also the Chinese way of doing things.

Bureaucratic delays and the following of precedents all contribute to a slower process. The Chinese side may not have approval to conclude the agreement—it is critical that you find out if they have authority, otherwise your negotiations will be fruitless. Another reason for slowness is poor information-gathering and communications infrastructure. The Chinese team, like its counterpart, may represent a variety of stakeholders with such intra-party negotiations complicating the pace and substance of the talks, often hidden to the foreign counterpart. The remedy is to use go-betweens to find out what the problems are, and to discover the issues and the personalities involved.

Some negotiations can be delayed or go nowhere because the Chinese are reluctant to say a clear "no," or to admit they made a mistake, or do not understand the economics of the situation. And the project can get bogged down if it is not a high priority for the Chinese government.

Another problem can be the language issue as both sides use interpreters and translators, which can be faulty and cause problems. Often, each side's interpreters will put common terms into both languages. In addition, there can be misunderstandings when each side forgets negotiations etiquette and speaks to the interpreter rather than to the person who is the business representative. Also, subtleties in one language may not be translated into the other. For example, phrases such as "Suppose we were to try this..." or "I see what your problem is..." when translated can sound aggressive rather than searching for common agreement.

Other frustrations can include a different approach to time and a desire for many details. In the terms of contract discussion stage, the Chinese will ask for arbitration in Chinese and that it be held in Beijing; this will become an important negotiation issue since arbitration in a third country could be more desirable. There may also be "tit for tat" or "quid pro quo" so that if the negotiation says that delays by the Chinese in payment will incur interest, the Chinese might respond that delays by foreign workers (arriving late) could be deducted from the total payments.

The contract signing phase requires consultation as well since the terms may have changed—thus the negotiator must carefully check the language again and again before signing. Also, be ready for the last-minute request for a new item or change, and then to decide when enough is enough. Who has the most to lose if the contract isn't signed? The forcing strategy of walking out on the deal at the last minute because of new terms must be carefully evaluated. Here the use of a go-between would be very helpful.

Lastly, the post-contract negotiation stage is mentioned because the fact that an agreement is reached and a contract signed doesn't mean that it is fixed and will be implemented as written. The contract can be seen in China (and in many Middle Eastern countries) as a stepping stone in an on-going relationship. The Chinese may soon request clarification meetings at which they will

Excellent negotiation resources on the web include:
www.globalnegotiationresources.com
www.getcustoms.com
www.globalnegotiationbook.com

demand more than is stated in the contract, or make additional demands. The way to handle this is to expect renegotiation; it may require more people onsite to insist very early that a supervising person or committee take responsibility for the Chinese side and the implementation of the contract. Another is to build-in a percentage for unforeseen costs into the total costs, or break the contract into stages of implementation with each successive stage dependent on the completion of the earlier one.

Lothar Katz, who is the author of *Negotiating International Business*, published by BookSurge (2ⁿᵈ edition, 2007), has posted a number of reports on the negotiating styles of fifty countries at the website www.globalnegotiationresources.com. At that site, click on the flag for whatever country you want to learn about, and you will be able to read that information online or download it as a PDF file. With an estimated 195 countries in the world, and even a listing for the negotiating styles for fifty of those countries at this website, it is unrealistic to master the information about every single country. Information on the cultural distinctions for a country also is available through well-regarded guides, such as *Kiss, Bow, or Shake Hands*, by Terri Morrison, Wayne A. Conaway, and George A. Borden, which covers doing business in sixty countries including what to expect in negotiations. The authors also have a website, www.getcustoms.com, which provides information on the latest edition of their book. They also offer a selection of free related articles, including "Negotiating in Different Cultures," by Morrison and Conaway. Their four suggestions in that article are:

- Never underestimate your prospect.
- Don't expect decisions to be made based upon your priorities.
- Be prepared to be tested by your foreign counterparts.
- Prepare yourself for unexpected negotiation techniques.

I suggest that those cultural distinctions are just part of the negotiation considerations when you are doing business internationally. In addition to any cultural differences, the questions that must be answered in all negotiations are:

1. Do the people at the table have the authority to settle this matter? If not, do they have recommending authority? And if not, who does have authority?

2. What deadlines are both sides facing and how does that leverage this negotiation?

3. What pressures are on both sides in terms of time, money, competition, etc.?

4. What would a good settlement look like?

5. What is the best alternative if no agreement is reached for your side and for theirs (away from the table)?

6. What is the worst alternative if no agreement is reached for your side and for theirs?

7. What mechanisms are necessary for the implementation and enforcement of this agreement?

8. How will this agreement be communicated? Must it be voted by a board of directors? A union membership? A board of trustees? Will there be a joint statement to all employees? To the press? To the community?

There is a new profession called a Negotiation Coach—these are professionals who know the ins and outs of these processes and who work with negotiating teams from various companies, both within and between countries. These coaches look at personal traits as well as institutional concerns for advice; some may even videotape the clients so they see how they come across. Others will provide guidelines for working with translators and interpreters. Others will discuss the strategies of creating a framework agreement where the concepts can be worked on and the details resolved later. If you are planning to do a lot of contracts internationally, and negotiating is a skill that you could use some help with, you might consider hiring a negotiating coach to help you master the techniques that will serve you and your business well.

## BASIC NEGOTIATING STYLES

Not all negotiation styles are alike and some negotiations are more about problem-solving than deal-making. When we go into another culture, for example, to a bazaar in the Middle East, we may engage in the ritual of bargaining that is often called "haggling" where each side does not expect the very first offer or demand to be the final offer and there is a respect for each party's acumen in driving the best bargain.

The negotiation assumes significance beyond the mere buying and selling and can be entertainment as well. In some cultures, the price tag may not mean the final price because it is subject to negotiations and the customer feels that he or she has been taken advantage of if the price tag becomes the final price. In other cultures, a consumer may expect to pay the price listed and instead of bargaining over terms, payments, etc. will go to another store to see if that price is lower.

If you are not comfortable with "haggling," you may fail to achieve the best price or terms because you want to avoid a potential confrontation. This is one indication of how some people feel about negotiations: vaguely uncomfortable or unsure. The best way to understand negotiations is to understand your own style, and your own approach to conflict. If you don't know what your "default position" is—how you usually respond to conflict—you will have some difficulties both in devising strategies and tactics in any negotiations, and in understanding the approaches used by your counterparts in other countries.

How do you know your own negotiating style? There are a variety of tests you can take. The most common was developed by Thomas-Kilmann Conflict Mode Instrument (TKI) which requires you to make thirty behavior choices that stem from each of the five negotiating style categories:

1. Competing

2. Collaborating

3. Compromising

4. Accommodating

5. Avoiding

We all have some aspect of each of these negotiating approaches but one is usually more dominant than the others. Dominance is determined by your level of concern for the issues and the winning of those issues, and your level of concern for the relationship and for keeping that on track.

Look over each of the five negotiating approaches that follow, and see if you can recognize yourself in those types.

## THE COMPETING NEGOTIATOR

With a competitive negotiator, the deal is the most important thing and the relationship is secondary. The competitive strategy is what many think of when the term "negotiations" is used. Indeed, high competitors as well as high collaborators enjoy negotiating but for different reasons. For the competitor, it is a chance to win and the competitor looks to deadlines, tactics such as opening moves, bargaining power and leverage, and may not be as concerned about the relationship with the other party.

This may have disastrous results if the loser in the negotiations feels coerced, abused, taken advantage of, or vanquished, and subsequently looks for a form of economic revenge or retribution. A potential limitation to the competitor strategy is looking at only what can be quantified by the deal and missing the intangibles that may be just as important such as "good will" and employee or customer loyalty. Donald Trump personifies the competitive negotiator.

## THE COLLABORATIVE NEGOTIATOR

When asked to describe a cooperative or collaborative negotiator, where the relationship is critical, we might think of South Africa's first Black President, Nelson Mandela, who worked toward the reconciliation of both whites and blacks. He used such symbols as winning the rugby World Cup in 1995 as one step toward accomplishing that goal, as can be seen in the 2009 film, *Invictus.* Collaborating is used in team building and working on common problems.

The collaborative negotiator tries to go underneath any stated "positions" by the other side to understand what the "interests" and "needs" are of both parties, and looks to see how those can be achieved. This negotiator also determines what items are not critical to one side but may be very important to the other and thus could be exchanged for a suitable agreement. The skills involved in collaboration negotiation involve patience, tact, questioning, and large exchanges of information. This approach to bargaining works when both sides trust each other, and can each see a common threat and one or more ways to work together to achieve mutual gains. Such approaches as "brainstorming" ideas, using flow charts and outside experts to make presentations are very effective for the collaborating negotiator. However, if this negotiator meets someone who is not predisposed to this approach, there may delays by the other side, especially if there is a disagreement over the agenda and goals.

While competitors may call negotiations "a game," collaborators may call it "a dance" whereby both sides are there to solve problems and build trust. The shortcomings to a collaborator's perspective may be working too hard to reach a resolution, and giving in to the competitor. The collaborator must also keep in mind the end result of the negotiation and whether an agreement can be reached, implemented and maintained, and what methods are available for amending or changing it.

Indeed, the collaborative style is the closest to the "Getting to Yes" approach of interest-based bargaining that was first researched by Professors Walton and Mckersie and then popularized by Harvard professors Roger Fisher and William Ury. This problem-solving approach concentrates on the issues rather than the personalities, going beneath the stated positions to determine the underlying interests and then reframing the problem to reflect those interests. The approach also uses brainstorming to generate options by both sides for mutual gain, and establishes objective standards by which to judge those options. This approach has been used in training and in many college, law, and business school negotiation courses. However, its application to the real world is still limited; it works best when both parties undergo joint pre-negotiation training in the goals, objectives and skills of this technique.

We hear of such success stories as the five-year agreement negotiated between American health care provider Kaiser-Permanente and its fifteen unions using this approach that dealt with working conditions, wages, and related topics. We also hear of mediators in various countries who work with both sides, seeing what interests they have in common, and then helping to broker a deal.

## THE ACCOMMODATING NEGOTIATOR

If you are an accommodator, you negotiate with an aim toward building relationships and making sure that problem-solving approaches are used to satisfy both sides. Unfortunately, if you are too accommodating, you may end up not having your goals realized and your approach may be viewed by a competitive person as one of weakness.

## THE COMPROMISING NEGOTIATOR

If you are a compromiser and that is the type of resolution that you feel comfortable working toward, then you look to close the gap between two offers, and for standards to achieve this closure quickly. The problem with compromising is that sometimes the compromiser may sacrifice finding a better result because not enough time or discussion has been allocated for that understanding. Indeed, a person who refuses to compromise may be considered either stubborn or principled, and the negotiation may end at an impasse with no agreement reached.

## THE AVOIDANCE NEGOTIATOR

The last approach is what's called the avoidance negotiator who does whatever they can to avoid conflict. Negotiators who practice this approach do not like confrontation and are very reluctant bargainers. While this approach may be useful if one side requires more information or the timing is wrong for the discussion, it can also result in no deal being made or some other party getting there first. People who are conflict avoiders may use hired agents to negotiate for them, or choose mechanisms that reduce face-to-face confrontations, such as e-mail or memos. While avoiders may display a great deal of tact in dealing with their more competitive or confrontational negotiators, they also may not be explicit enough about what their goals are for the negotiation and thus lose out.

# Negotiating Tactics

Now that you know the five approaches to negotiating and have determined your style, it's time to consider various negotiating tactics you may encounter.

## "GOOD COP, BAD COP"

In this situation, two people are involved in the negotiations with one person pointing out all the positives, and the other person pointing out the negatives. The technique is manipulative because it causes the person who is on the receiving side of the negotiations to feel that he or she has an ally in the "good cop." However, both the good cop and the bad cop, in this negotiating technique, are out to get the best deal for themselves.

## LYING AND OTHER DECEPTIVE TECHNIQUES

There are some unethical dealmakers who will lie. They will embellish statistics, alter profit and loss statements, or exaggerate the success of a particular product or service. If they don't lie outright about such crucial matters, they will leave out vital information hoping you won't ask for it. And even if you do ask for it, you might get an answer that is a lie.

Other deceptive techniques include: displaying false non-verbal messages to throw off the other side; and making false concessions or demands just to make the other side feel as if they have gotten a better deal when those concerns are meaningless.

What can you do about this? First, you need to do your homework and make sure you are getting information from a reliable third party. Don't expect those with a reputation for lying or withholding information to give you what you need to negotiate in your own best interest. You might even have to pay a local third party to find out the information that you need to negotiate with your strongest position—having accurate and real statistics.

The investment in doing so might be well worth it, especially if a deal is potentially lucrative. Second, even if you know the other party is lying, be careful about confronting others in the negotiation with this fact. If their culture permits and even encourages lying in business, not only could they be offended but they might deny it anyway and then you can get into a spitting match and have the whole deal fall through.

Years ago, President Ronald Reagan was quoted as saying, "Trust, but verify" when he was describing nuclear disarmament negotiations with the Russians; that approach is just as true today. Whenever a negotiator says, "I wouldn't lie to you..." or "trust me..." that is the time to keep your antennae up and to be ready to challenge their approach or offers, but in a polite way. Point out the inconsistencies with what is said today with what was said yesterday or the previous week. It helps if you have notes as well as an observer with you. In addition, it is helpful if you can "initial" a tentative agreement on certain points so that you don't need to revisit them.

There are differences between mere "puffing" and "exaggerating" and outright lies, and many negotiators expect some exaggerations in their exchanges. Indeed, that is why many conflict-avoiding individuals do not relish being on a negotiating team or facing an adversary. However, preparation, knowledge, independent sources, and a determined approach that keeps coming back to the common goals, will help. Also, there is negotiating language to put in a contract that will verify numbers, performance standards, and completion. Therefore, if there is a dispute later on, it might go to an independent but knowledgeable arbitrator rather than the courts in various foreign jurisdictions.

Again, trust your knowledge of the other negotiator's reputation and if it is one of fooling the other side, be very careful and cautious and make sure that your side writes up the final agreement. There have been instances when new clauses or phrases are somehow inserted into the final agreement because it was written by the other side. Either have a joint drafting committee or do it yourself because the temptation to err on the side of advantages is very great.

Make sure that terms are defined in both or many languages with examples so there is no misunderstanding of when the project is to be completed, when the bill is to be paid, by how much and in what currency and deposited in what bank, etc. No detail is too small. Even if the agreement is a framework agreement, before final signature, make sure that the key terms are included and checked and rechecked.

More can be lost by a misplaced comma than you can imagine. Another tactic that helps is saying you're sorry if there is a mistake and that you are working to correct it. Plan in advance that some typos, errors in proofreading or translations, etc. might occur. Have joint committees (one from each side) review the document to make sure all mistakes are corrected.

## ENJOYING THE BARGAINING GAME (OR DANCE)

Most cultures expect to bargain in deal negotiations and, in fact, some cultures, such as Spain's, enjoy the bargaining. Know that about a culture so you can begin with a much higher anticipated amount than you think you'll get and bargain from there. If you start with the final amount you think you will get in the deal, you'll frequently be disappointed because the bargaining will have nowhere to go. Some cultures expect as much as a 20-30% difference between an initial offer and the final negotiated deal. Get comfortable with bargaining, especially asking for more. You may be surprised how frequently you actually get it! Conversely, if you do not ask for a certain amount or item, you will probably never get it. It is helpful to have a reason behind every offer and counteroffer and to explain how that offer or counter was derived, using past practices, formulas, going rates, accepted approaches, productivity, etc. These reasons can go a long way in convincing the other side of your genuine interest in reaching a settlement.

## "TAKE IT OR LEAVE IT"

"Here's the offer, take it or leave it." This is the most common style in the United States with those who are not skilled negotiators. That is why it is often best to bring in a trained negotiator to do a deal. The money you invest in the expert negotiator is often offset by the increase in revenue that they are able to generate. What's the worst that can happen if you or your negotiator asks for more money and someone says "no"? You will still be able to decide whether you will accept or decline the original offer. It is rare that the buyer would cancel a deal just because you ask for more. Or, you may still be able to broker a compromise.

This is what professional dealmakers and negotiators will do for you. They are comfortable with the negotiating process. Most work on commission basis so it's a win-win arrangement. They will hopefully get you a higher price so their commission will basically be paid for out of that higher price. If you are not comfortable doing negotiations for yourself, either find someone who can do it for you, or accept that you are, in general, getting less money for your deals than you should be getting.

## COOPERATION

This negotiating style sees the process in a very systematic way. Information is gathered about what is being sold and then, once all the questions are answered about what is at stake, a deal is offered. You tell the buyer or the other side what you want; they tell you what they want; and you come to terms. It still can be a long and involved process, especially if lawyers are involved, but the negotiations are polite and respectful. No manipulative or aggressive tactics are used such as yelling, kicking, or chair throwing.

## PRETENDING DISINTEREST

Often the person who is very interested in the deal pretends to be disinterested in order to get the other side to offer their goods or services at a lower price.  It is often hard to detect whether or not the disinterest is genuine.  What should you do if you are faced with this as a negotiating tactic? First, act as disinterested as they are and see what happens. Second, countermanding this tactic is to have two or three additional real background offers you could turn to so they do not gain the upper hand by professing lack of interest. Third, "watch their feet" and see if anything they have said or done before this phase of the negotiations substantiates whether they have real interest or not since you will have a stronger negotiating position if they are actually keen for the deal.

145

Be very careful with this negotiating tactic. It can backfire, especially if you're the seller feigning disinterest and the buyer, believing that you do not wish to go forward with a deal, buys another product or hires someone else instead. So, while this tactic could get you a better price if it is used cautiously and carefully, it also could unwittingly cost you the entire deal. The Catch-22 is that it is human nature to want someone to be enthusiastic about doing business together, to making a deal, but it is also a potentially unwise business strategy to act too excited about buying or selling or the price could go up, or other key terms could get that much harder to achieve.

## USING TIME TO GET WHAT YOU WANT

Time can be used as a negotiating strategy. You can suggest that you need a decision by a certain time to help move the negotiations along, or you can ask for more time to decide as a way to diffuse the interest in a deal in the hope that this will enable you to come in with a lower offer. Some cultures have distinctive attitudes toward time when it comes to negotiations: while the initial agreement may be reached quickly, it may take much longer to get the written contracts signed. Trying to speed the process along could hurt the current relationship and the hope of any additional future negotiations.

Another tactic is to drag out the negotiations for such a long time that the other side thinks the deal is dead and no longer viable. But when the other party gets back to the seller (or buyer) and offers to finalize the deal, the one who has waited so long and who has written off the deal as dead in the water can now be "tricked" into caving in and saying "yes" because they have been worn down by the wait. They are now so happy a deal is finally going to happen that they are far less sharp or demanding as they were all those hours, months, weeks, or even years before when the parties first started discussing the deal.

# *Techniques that Rarely Work*

## SHOW OF FORCE

Kicking a trash can across the room during contract negotiations used to be a common occurrence by a negotiator trying to show that he wasn't going to get talked down in talks between a publishing company and the unions. He used anger as an intimidation tactic. It also revealed how frustrated he had become because the contract talks weren't going anywhere. But it usually did little to resolve anything.

Another way to show force is through words, whether verbal or written. Once again, this usually backfires. It might feel good to discharge all that fury with specific words that express disgust or anger as well as through a loud tone of voice, or by writing words that similarly convey the party's annoyance, even in a witty or eloquent way, but if the words "cross the line," they can sabotage the entire deal by causing the other side to sever rather than expedite the negotiations.

## BEING AGGRESSIVE OR PUSHY

This tactic will backfire if it is utilized during negotiations in many cultures, especially Japan and Australia. As journalist Misako Hida, who is from Japan but who now lives and works in New York City, points out, "They don't appreciate an aggressive and pushy negotiating style." Ditto for the Australians.

# CHAPTER 9

# Contracts and Getting Paid[1]

Acontract is an agreement by two parties to do business together according to the terms that are stipulated in the deal. Contracts can be as simple as an oral agreement, followed by a handshake, or as complicated as a thirty-page detailed document. Most contracts fall somewhere in-between, such as a letter of agreement, which is a shorter and simplified type of contract.

In certain countries and cultures, as in the United Kingdom, a handshake and a verbal agreement are honored but are not considered legally binding. You might want to follow up such an informal pact with a written agreement.

The information in this chapter is not meant to substitute for the advice of a lawyer. Contracts typically will be negotiated between lawyers with one of those lawyers representing your interests; or through an agent who, although not a lawyer, has training and experience dealing in your particular business. Some companies, especially entrepreneurs, small businesses, or consultants, may not feel they have the funds to hire a lawyer to negotiate a contract on their behalf. And, although most agents work on a commission basis, the amount of money involved in some business dealings may not be large enough for an agent to pursue.

## CONTRACT BASICS

What follows is a list of some of the very basic concerns that a contract should address. However, once again, if at all possible, consult a lawyer or a trained agent with expertise in your particular business or field for help with the specific contracts for your international business issues.

---

[1] This chapter is for general information only. It is not meant to be a substitute for professional legal advice. If you have any specific legal questions or concerns, consult an attorney.

## WHO SHOULD SIGN THE CONTRACT?

In the United States, we are used to attorneys drafting the contracts and assisting in their negotiations with final approval by the heads of the companies involved. However, in many countries, it is the business leaders who do the negotiating with the lawyers as advisors, and it is the business leaders who sign the agreement. Make sure that if you do enter into a contract with someone that he or she has the authority to sign the contract on behalf of that company. For example, an officer of the company, such as a president or CEO, may have to sign the contract. If a lower-level employee signed it, their authority might not hold up if anything about the terms of the deal were to be called into question later on.

It is always important to get legal counsel before signing a contract or agreement with a foreign customer or business.

## DO YOU NEED SOMEONE TO WITNESS IT?

Witnesses are important depending upon the jurisdiction where the contract is negotiated as well as where it will be enforced. Many more companies are negotiating international agreements that have arbitration as the method of enforcement but even here, there may be a requirement that the contract be witnessed. Attesting to the signature of the parties becomes important during any claim of breach of the agreement; and, having witnesses further validates the transaction. Again, check the law of the country or countries that will be involved in the enforcement of each agreement.

## WHAT POINTS SHOULD
## THE CONTRACT COVER?

Any contract dealing with another country for a service or product should be specific. Typical contracts specify what is required and expected of both sides, as wells as when, how many, where, what costs, and, if there is a delay, what defines "delay," and what corrective measures must be taken. If you think about what could possibly go wrong and make a check-list, then you can go backwards and create a contract that covers those contingencies.

Just be aware that there is no way to predict everything and "Acts of God" do occur. Include a clause that addresses what to do in the wake of an unforeseen event that is not covered by the agreement, or if there is a problem in interpretation or enforcement. This clause would provide for additional arbitration and spell out which country, court, and law will cover the translation, and which language(s) will be involved. *It is critical to have local counsel from that country involved so that the contract is enforceable and workable.* Also, there is probably a business community with its own employer association or council that gives advice and explains the prevailing business practice for a specific industry, product market, etc.

The contract should specify the product or service that is being sold or provided and what fee is to be paid for that product or service, and it should also indicate the agreed upon recourse if the contract is breached. The date on the contract should be decided as to its meaning: is it the date both sides sign it? Is it the date it is received by both sides? Is it the date that actions begin as described in the agreement?

Also, when looking at the duration of the contract, check to see what is the usual and customary length, how each side can terminate, amend or change the agreement (what kind of notice is needed and timeframe) and addresses what happens when the contract expires. Is there a presumption that it will continue unless one or both sides says otherwise, or do the parties have to affirmatively renegotiate, re-sign, or re-do the agreement?

This also goes to the question of how long the contract is in effect. Depending on the product cycle, the contract may be short- or long-term, and there may need to be provisions if the price of the product fluctuates, delivery is impacted, etc. Indeed, what happens if the contract goes past the expiration date? In some agreements, it means that all terms and conditions continue until the contract is re-negotiated. In other agreements, when the contract terminates, then the terms cease. This is an important situation for all contract drafters to discuss well in advance, especially if there is a possibility that the firm could be sold, merged or acquired, or a major disruption could occur in the product market, fiscal market, currency market, in fact anything in the world marketplace.

Lawyers for each party will also check that any copyright concerns or IP (intellectual property) issues are addressed and/or protected by this contract. Again, checking what the law in the jurisdictions covers as well as what rights each party would like preserved in the contract that could be enforced through arbitration should be considered before signing the agreement. This becomes very important for joint ventures and when a start-up company wants to increase its market share and there may be competition with the other company.

As mentioned earlier, the contract drafters ought to consider what state or country to list as the place where the contract is being drawn up, and address the question: "is it better to have the contract drawn up in your state or country rather than that of the international business with which you are signing the contract?"

In a number of countries, the parties may feel that they must use local courts and arbitrators and in certain countries, such as China, they may be forced to do so. However, there is a trend toward the use of international arbitration. Indeed, while international arbitration offers speed, informality, and economy, the growth of this field is really explained by the desire by each party to avoid having their case determined in a foreign judicial forum. This is because one party may be unfamiliar with that country's court procedures, judges, language, or bias and neither party wishes to be judged in the other's backyard. This is also true because there is no multilateral convention for the recognition of foreign judgments and few bilateral treaties, either.

An international mechanism for the enforcement of foreign arbitral awards, called the New York Convention, is the Convention on the Recognition and Enforcement of Foreign Arbitration Awards. It went into effect in 1958 and established a system which recognizes the arbitral awards of member countries rendered abroad, and excludes judicial review of the merits of the arbitral award by the court where enforcement is sought. The New York Convention was designed to give international currency to arbitration awards and any award rendered binding in a New York Convention country can, under the Convention, be enforced in any other New York Convention signatory. The Convention does not provide an international mechanism to ensure the validity of the award where rendered; this was left to the provisions of local law.

The private international dispute resolution system (arbitration) is responsible for the increase in world trade, investment, finance, and technological developments. International arbitration works because of national arbitration legislation, international conventions and treaties. Several institutions, such as the International Chamber of Commerce (ICC), administer international commercial arbitration proceedings with experienced advocates and arbitrators. Other rules include the UNCITRAL (United Nations Convention on the Recognition and Enforcement of Foreign Arbitration Awards) in 1985 which fashioned a Model Law on International Commercial Arbitration.

In addition to arbitration, there are other alternative dispute resolution procedures that should be considered, ranging from mediation (a neutral process that is not binding) to early neutral evaluation (a process by which an expert gives his/her opinion of how the case will likely be settled in court); mediation-arbitration (a combined process whereby sometimes the same individual hears the case and then, if there is no voluntary resolution, makes a final and binding determination); fact-finding with recommendation (a panel investigates the dispute and issues recommendations on its settlement); a "mini-trial" (both sides prepare their cases and submit them to a neutral party for resolution of what has also been called a "structured settlement negotiation" for complex cases); or "summary jury trial" (attorneys for both sides put on an abbreviated case to one or more juries who may give an advisory verdict which may be used to settle the case).

There are international organizations that provide neutral players for these types of commercial disputes, as well as for helping to determine the language to be used, fees to be paid, the hearing's location, time limits, etc. All of these factors should be investigated in advance of signing the contract. Other mechanisms that may be considered include the use of an Ombudsman to receive complaints and help to facilitate their resolution within the organization. Ombudsmen are individuals specially selected to assist many hospitals, franchises, government agencies, and others to deal with complaints, and/or resolve employee and workplace issues.

## CHANGING A SIGNED CONTRACT

There are cultures where revising a contract after it has been signed is not as horrifying a thought as it may seem to most Americans who usually see signed contracts as chiseled in stone. In some cultures, it is even okay to renegotiate a signed written agreement. For example, Lothar Katz, in *Negotiating International Business*, notes that the Japanese do not view signed contracts as final agreements since their expectation is that both sides remain flexible if conditions change, which may include agreeing to modify contract terms.

But, in general, this doesn't happen often. Assume that whatever you agree to is what will be expected. Therefore you need to be very careful about what you sign, and make sure you are clear on every single point of the agreement. When any contract has been signed and countersigned, the request that the contract be amended because the terms were not correct, or even what was agreed to, could easily be ignored—which the other party has a right to do since everyone should be in complete agreement with the contract at the point when it is signed. Make sure you read every line in the contract since the terms will directly impact you and your business.

If you do try to change the terms of the contract after it has been signed, do not worry about whether or not this is seen in a negative light by the other party. If you have good reasons for suggesting the changes, even if they decide not to honor your requests, as long as the business proves to be mutually beneficial they are probably not going to hold it against you that you asked for those changes.

## FAILING TO ALTER THE MASTER CONTRACT EVEN AFTER CHANGES HAVE BEEN AGREED UPON

In this dubious practice, you and the party with whom you are negotiating mark up the original contract and you, in good faith, sign the final contract, making the assumption that the agreed upon changes have been transferred to the final document. It is only down the road, when a problem might arise, that you go to the final, signed contract, only to discover that some or all of the changes had never been added or were deleted from the final master contract. That is why some companies ask that all changes being made to a contract are indicated in boldface type and that each change is initialed by both parties, and that the final contract is checked against previous versions to make sure that it is indeed the revised contract that everyone has agreed to. You might, to be careful, want to keep the various versions of the contract, comparing each earlier version to the latest one, making sure it is to everyone's satisfaction.

This tactic rarely works and usually backfires because someone will discover the discrepancies in the contracts and this could lead to bad feelings between the parties, being labeled dishonest, or even canceling the deal all together. If you detect that the other party has intentionally doctored the contracts, especially if it is in their favor, proceed cautiously in your dealings with them, even if they apologize and make the necessary changes.

## GETTING PAID

Now that you have established international business relationships and are beginning to sell your products or services in other countries, it's time to turn your attention to one of the most important aspects of any business relationship: getting paid. You may have assumed that when a deal has been agreed upon, payment would be forthcoming. And that usually is the case. Just be aware that when doing business internationally, it can be more difficult to get paid for your goods or services. And, it is simply not cost effective to get on a plane and spend possibly thousands of dollars to travel to another part of the world to try to collect the money you were promised.

How can you avoid these unfortunate situations? One of the best solutions is to use trusted local distributors or agents. One of their responsibilities is to help you get paid if you are an entrepreneur or small business. They will step in and contact the local business or individuals who owe you

*When doing business internationally it is useful to know if the country you are dealing with does business mainly with cash or if they also use credit or debit cards.*

money. Chances are they know the business that owes you money, either from establishing similar relationships for other foreigners or from business associations to which they belong.

When doing business internationally it is useful to know if the country you are dealing with does business mainly with cash or if they also use credit or debit cards. There are some who find global business better than domestic because of the practices that often go with it. For example, Julie Austin, the inventor of a patented wrist water bottle, Swiggies, notes: "I do business in almost every country in the world. I prefer doing international business because they all know it has to be money up front, or at least 50% up front and 50% on delivery." She even prefers not to ship her goods until she has been paid in full.

When I was in Auckland, New Zealand I met a speaker and coach who told me how she and a fellow trainer went to Nigeria to conduct seminars. They were unprepared for the fact that Nigeria is a cash-only culture. They expected to pay for their hotel with a credit card but cash was expected. They got their hotel and airfare covered by the company that hired them but it took over two years to get "most of what they owed us. But at least they made a serious attempt to honor their commitment."

Getting paid in advance is usually the best way to ensure you will receive the money promised when doing business internationally. However, it is often difficult to get your buyer to agree to this. Sometimes you can get an agreement for 50% of the fee or purchase price up front and the balance upon receipt of the goods or delivery of your services or, alternatively, within thirty days from the bill-of-lading date. Payment in advance can be made by direct deposit into your corporate bank account. Two other options are PayPal, or American Express FX International Payments.

As mentioned earlier, another good method is to use local distributors or agents who have proven track records and verifiable references. They not only handle the deal for you, but collect any monies due on your behalf. For that service the local distributor or agent will get either a flat fee or a percentage of the deal. They usually work on a commission basis; they collect the money, take out their commission, and send you the rest, minus any withholding tax for a particular country, if any.

Once again, protocol is a factor. Ask the person with whom you are doing business about their preferred method of payment. They probably have experience with international transactions and may have a system already worked out. Just make sure it is not going to make you incur a financial loss or have to wait excessively long. Work any payment schedule out as part of the negotiation process. That way, getting paid will not become a bone of contention that could threaten the international business relationship you worked so hard to establish.

## FORMS 8802 AND 6166

If you are an American company and you have made a deal with a foreign company, you will usually have the agreed upon fee you are to be paid taxed by that government before you get your payment. If you have what is known as a Certificate of Residency that is issued by the IRS of the United States, showing that you pay taxes in the United States, you can avoid what is known as double taxation, whereby you are taxed at a higher rate by the foreign company. Although requesting Form 6166 used to be done rather informally—you or your accountant wrote to the IRS office handling these requests and, within a few months, you received a Certificate of Residency for each country that you'd requested—a few years ago, the system became automated. Now you have to request the 6166 form by filling out the 8802 form online and paying the $35 required fee which covers up to twenty letters/6166 forms, with each different country requiring its own letter.

Once you pay the fee and send in the electronic request, the IRS has 30-45 days to respond. You may find that your initial query leads to a request for further information that you or your accountant need to supply, resulting in an additional waiting period after you provide the follow-up materials.

Some international companies will allow you to simply pay the higher tax charges so that what monies you get for the deal are thereby reduced by those additional taxes. Others require you to use Form 6166.

Patience is the main protocol skill that is necessary for awaiting the necessary Certificate of Residency form that will enable you to get paid in certain countries.

Furthermore, a new Certificate of Residency will be required for each year that you are receiving revenues from particular foreign companies or countries. You cannot use the same letter from year to year. You also cannot apply for the form for the current year until your tax return for that year has been filed with the IRS by March 15th, for a corporate return, and by April 15th, for a personal one.

During the time that you are awaiting the necessary Form 6166 or Certificate of Residency letter, keep a positive attitude about your project or sales moving forward. You have the right to withhold your services or products until you are paid; however, you need to explain this to your business colleague in a way that does not offend them or sabotage the deal going forward as you await the necessary paperwork.

# CHAPTER 10

# Summing Up

One of the key lessons I have learned from my own international business experiences was to become much more sensitive to the benefits of spending more time in person with global business connections, whether in their home countries, or if they visit my native America.

Because we are all so busy, we have come to depend on trade shows as a more time and cost efficient way of connecting to people around the world. On the surface, it seems like an effective solution for meeting and pitching to a multitude of potential international buyers (or sellers) in the shortest time period. But I call those trade shows the business version of "speed dating" where singles meet a plethora of potential suitors in just seven or eight minutes and make quick decisions about whether to take that brief encounter to the next level and go on an actual date.

The half hour to an hour appointment that you might have with a new potential business partner at a trade show is not nearly enough time to get to know each other's culture, the uniqueness of who you are, or your potential business partner. But it's definitely a start and better than just communicating via the Internet; you can always follow up your initial meeting at a trade show with longer meetings or even sharing a meal together either in their country or yours as well as additional phone and e-mail communications in-between your in-person visits.

You can intensify your international *Grow Global* efforts even further by continuing to attend trade shows, perhaps even adding another show or two in different locations in the years ahead, but also by spending more time and effort going to the physical places where your current business partners, clients, customers, or local agents live. Here is an example of the progression in a potential business relationship —and possibly even a personal friendship —from a trade show initial meeting. Year 1: Meet at the trade show in another country for a half-hour appointment. Year 2: Meet at the same trade show for dinner, spending more time together, getting to know each other and your respective businesses. Year 2/4 months later: Meet for dinner with other business associates and friends in the country of that potential business partner/friend. Here is the e-mail I received from this colleague as the time of my trip to her native Taiwan drew closer: "Great. See you soon. Welcome to my city, my country."

Of course traveling internationally involves an investment of time as well as money and sometimes that is just not in the budget now or in the foreseeable future. Fortunately, there is still that old-fashioned but useful way to connect besides the internet known as the telephone or the Internet-based phone-like services such as Skype. By starting to pick up the phone again, or using Skype or similar services, whether for just audio or for videoconferencing as well, rather than just sending an e-mail or text message, you have the ability to add more texture to your communications as non-verbal cues, such as pauses and voice quality and volume, become a factor and not just the written words in an e-mail.

Even with language challenges, connecting by phone is more of a two-way interaction than just communicating by text. As noted above, you get to share more about each other through your voice including your tone, pauses, and even your breathing and, if you use a web cam, through your body language including facial expressions.

While this book touched upon many international protocol issues, it's up to you to know and master the protocol of your own culture. You want to be the best of what you are.

Remember, you do not need to "act" like a local, you just need to "know" and respect local customs, protocol and attitudes. Focus on how your cultures are similar while acknowledging the differences and don't let those contrasts sabotage your work or personal relationships.

Dr. Rachna Kumar, who teaches international business and has clients around the world, reminds us of the importance of dealing with gender differences in other cultures. She says that being sensitive to those differences will help you in designing the right team for international business.

In Dubai, China, and Mexico, for example, Dr. Kumar says that it is better to have a team that includes a male and a female. In India today, that would not be necessary.

There are numerous books you can read to gather information about specific protocol issues related to a particular country. But what is in short supply are books about how important it is to have the right attitude, one that is respectful of other cultures, and curious about what is sacred and expected so as not to offend. So I leave you with this parting thought. Be the best of who you are—not a chameleon or clone of whatever culture you happen to be dealing with at that time. That will take you much further than worrying about the meaning of a specific gesture, or remembering all those holidays, or figuring out what negotiating style goes with what country. All are still useful to learn, but if you have an open and a curious mind, you can ask and find all that out.

Another key concept that I want to emphasize as you expand your business worldwide is to be mindful of those who contact *you* to initiate or follow-up a business connection. If time is an issue, try to delegate your response to a staff

> *Focus on how your cultures are similar while acknowledging the differences and don't let those contrasts sabotage your work or personal relationships.*

member, use student interns, or, as a last resort, use an "auto-responder" e-mail that thanks someone for contacting you and explains that you are away, busy, or whatever. In this way, you are honoring the person who took the time to contact you.

Connecting in a respectful and positive way, one on one, is the essence of international business protocol—the foundation of your success.

**

APPENDIX

# U.S. Government Regulations and Getting Help for Developing International Business*

The fact that the world has become interconnected in so many ways has made it much easier to do business in other countries, including many that were, until recently, very far off the beaten path, including the People's Republic of China and the former Soviet Union. At the same time, the decision to cross borders requires careful consideration because of government regulations and differing economic, social and cultural environments. This section will provide guidelines in finding international business opportunities from U.S Government and international organization sources.

## GETTING STARTED

The decision to go global should begin with an analysis of where the opportunities exist, or market research and analysis. Before you make your first trip abroad, spend the first dollar of advertising money, or ship the first package, you need to understand and quantify the business potential of overseas markets. Fortunately, a low-cost or no-cost resource is available: the U.S. Department of Commerce, through its International Trade Administration, offers virtually "one-stop shopping" for companies interested in going global.

The U.S. Department of Commerce's Foreign Commercial Service (FCS) stations officers at U.S. embassies around the world. They are there to assist U.S. businesses in finding markets for goods or services. These officers, supported by locally hired staff, will spend their time

*I wish to thank Judyt Mandel for her help in preparing this Appendix based on her 28 years of experience as a Foreign Service Officer with tours of duty in London and Moscow; she is currently an international business development consultant.

learning about the host country's laws and regulations, meeting with government and business leaders, and tracking industry and commercial developments throughout the country. They are ready and willing to meet with you or speak to you by phone or e-mail to share their knowledge and help you find buyers, identify potential partners or distributors, qualify investment opportunities, and assist you with problems that may arise in the course of doing business in that country. Usually this is a five-step process in which you:

1. Do research on the market or country in which you are interested.
2. Find customers or distributors.
3. Arrange to contact the individual or company concerned.
4. Strike a deal with them.
5. Arrange to ship your goods or provide your service.

The FCS makes this information available online as the Country Commercial Code for more than 80 countries around the world. It can be seen at http://www/BUYUSA.gov and navigating to the country or region in which you are interested.

## MARKET RESEARCH

The U.S. Foreign Commercial Service researches local conditions to find sectors and specific markets where U.S. exports stand a good chance of success. Its reports are organized by country or region, and market sector or sub sector (such as the transportation industry in Japan, or the market for hand tools in Brazil). They describe the conditions American or foreign exporters face, including the size of the market in dollar amounts, competitors, what a company must do to enter the market, and any peculiarities of doing business in the host country.

The Export.Gov website also posts notices of solicitations for certain goods and services being sought in the host country, such as a search for construction services to build a road or hospital, or providers of medical equipment to furnish a newly built facility. The range of goods and services covered by these reports is virtually unlimited from architectural services to zoo supplies. You can even sign up with the Department to receive e-mail notifications of international commercial conferences and exhibits, and upcoming visits by international delegations seeking U.S. goods and services or partnership opportunities.

The U.S. Department of Commerce also offers instructional materials for those interested in going global, including seminars and conferences that give you step by step guidance on going global. Its website, http://www.buyusa.gov, lists the time and place of these sessions which bring together U.S. Government export specialists and industry representatives willing to share their experience and best practices. If you cannot attend the sessions in person, there is the "webinar," an interactive teleconferencing tool that allows participants at widely different locations to exchange information and probe market opportunities, as well as to make contact with regional or national experts who can assist in business development activities in a selected part of the world. Many small- and medium-sized businesses have gotten the information and impetus to expand their business overseas from these government resources.

## ADVERTISING AND BRANDING

The Internet is a great tool for advertising your products or services, but how do you attract potential buyers to your site? A good way to let people know about your offerings is to participate in international trade fairs or professional conferences in your industry or sector. The Frankfurt Book Fair, held each October in Frankfurt, Germany, is a good example of such an event which brings together publishers, distributors and authors from over a hundred countries. Not only do the participants display their wares and upcoming offerings, they can check out what competitors around the world are producing, network with current or potential customers or partners from around the world, make deals on the spot, and reach out to the thousands of visitors who flock to the various halls and stands daily. The Canton Trade Fair held semi-annually in Guangzhou, China, is one of the largest such events in the world, and boasts that more than $66 million in deals were concluded there in 2009 in just a few days.

However, participation in a trade fair can be expensive. In addition to travel, hotel, meals and entertainment expenses, most exhibitors must invest in a booth or display that can cost thousands of dollars, and they may also need to hire personnel and possibly translators to staff their display area.

If your business is not ready to undertake that kind of investment, you can opt for a relatively inexpensive way to display your product by participating in a free or low-cost exhibit organized by the U.S. Department of Commerce to help companies to enter or expand in certain markets. You will be responsible for paying the cost of shipping your product to the address overseas provided by the U.S. Department of Commerce. For an additional, relatively modest fee, they will handle putting your product into the display as well as any catalog that they create for the show. Department of Commerce representatives will staff a booth at the fair, distribute the promotional materials that you provide, and will even obtain contact information so that you can follow up directly with potential customers.

You might also choose to advertise your company's product or service by buying a low-cost ad in the catalog distributed at the fair. This will include your advertising and logo, translated into the local language.

## FINDING RELIABLE
## CUSTOMERS AND PARTNERS

One of the most difficult aspects of going global is finding a reliable company with which to partner, or a customer who will live up to his or her obligations when you do not know them personally.  Start-up investor Esther Dyson lives in New York City but travels frequently especially to Russia, where she has been doing business since 1989. She says she would not do a transaction without going in person but would not advise someone to do a transaction at all without knowing with whom they are dealing.

Rather than taking a leap in the dark, you can turn to the U.S. Commercial Service of the U.S. Department of Commerce to assist you in finding and setting up meetings with firms that have been prequalified and prescreened, or with potential overseas agents, distributors, sales representatives and strategic business partners. As part of their fee-based "Gold Key" program, you will be provided with:

- Appointments with prescreened and prequalified firms in the country of interest

- Background and contact information on each potential partner

- Customized market briefing with U.S. Commercial Service staff

- Market research on the relevant industry sector

- Debriefing with U.S. Commercial staff to discuss results and plan follow-up action

- Meeting space (if an American Center in the host country is available for the date of visit)

- Logistical support, including hotel reservations and interpreter for meetings (paid directly by client in cash to the interpreter)

Before you take a risk in exporting or partnering with a foreign company or person, you should check their credentials, even if you cannot visit the country and meet in person. For a fee, the U.S. Commercial Service will perform "due diligence" on a company or individual in the host country, and provide you with an opinion as to the viability and reliability of that company or individual. The service is called an International Company Profile, and asks you to complete a simple questionnaire about the kind of information you are seeking. Local FCS representatives will check the company's or individual's financial information, compliance with local tax laws, whether there are any judgments pending against them, their reputation in the community, press reports about them, and any other information you need to make an informed decision about that company. This service can help you avoid potential disasters.

I was told about one case in which a U.S. defense contractor asked the FCS in New Delhi for a background check on a local company that proclaimed it had strong ties to the Indian Ministry of Defense. The U.S. firm was interested in a pending ammunition removal and abatement solicitation for the Indian Government. The U.S. Foreign Commercial Service representative found information implicating one of the partners in that company in a defense procurement scandal—a kiss of death for the procurement. The U.S. Company was warned in time to avoid an entangling partnership with that company.

As noted in Chapter 9, it is always useful to obtain legal counsel before you sign a contract or an agreement with a foreign customer or business.

The U.S. Commercial Service has 109 offices in cities around the United States dedicated to helping U.S. businesses go global. These offices are staffed by knowledgeable and experienced trade facilitators who can answer questions or provide additional assistance by telephone or in person. A listing of U.S. domestic offices can be found at:
http://www.buyusa.gov/home/us.html.

At that site, you can also find a listing of their international partners in 72 countries. The U.S. Commercial Service has specialists in a variety of industry, such as publishing. They also organize trade missions, usually lasting a week or so, to various regions which includes meetings with government and industry leaders and businesses looking to import goods from U.S. businesses. Webinars and teleconferences are sponsored that are industry or region specific; the U.S. Commercial Service also organizes bringing companies to trade shows around the world either through catalogue only participation or, if they have booth space, exhibiting of goods as well as providing a meeting place for appointments for those who are participating in a particular trade show. There are also in-person half-day or all-day seminars offered at local offices of the U.S. Commercial Service throughout the year.

Another good source of advice about doing business in a foreign country and finding a reliable local partner or supplier is through the local Chamber of Commerce or local business council. Most trading countries have a well developed Chamber of Commerce system which links the local business community and provides an easy entry to information about, and resources available to pursue business opportunities in that country. Many of those organizations have ties to the U.S. Chamber of Commerce's International Division or to a bilateral U.S.-country Business Council or Association which seeks to promote greater interchange between the U.S. and the country's business communities. Some active and well-known examples are the U.S. Russia Business Council, the U.S.-Libya Business Council, and the U.S.-Algeria Business Council. These organizations offer a variety of benefits to members, including the opportunity to participate in discussions of legislation and trade regulations affecting business with that country, meeting visiting government and business leaders, and identifying other businesses interested in, or doing business in the country in question. Often potential partners or sub-contractors can be found at such meetings.

Information about the reputation and standing of potential customers or clients can be ascertained through the informal networking that the organization provides. Many of these organizations also provide on-line search tools to facilitate contacts with counterpart member businesses, and can often assist in identifying local officials and organizations that can help with market entry. While most of these organizations require a paid membership in order to use the full array of services they provide, many will allow non-members to attend conferences or meetings and other events for a modest fee.

As noted in Chapter 2, having someone in another country that you can turn to for advice and information can be pivotal to an international experience that is manageable and positive versus one that is disastrous and regrettable.

## ADDITIONAL U.S. GOVERNMENT AND INTERNATIONAL BUSINESS SOURCES

The U.S. Trade and Development Agency, U.S. Agency for International Development, and the Millennium Challenge Corporation are major sources for U.S. Government-funded international business opportunities that offer relatively low-risk options for U.S. businesses interested in going global.

# THE U.S. TRADE
# DEVELOPMENT AGENCY (USTDA)

USTDA provides seed financing to stimulate U.S. sales of goods and services overseas, especially those that promote economic development in poor and medium income countries around the world. USTDA tries to bridge the gap between traditional foreign assistance and U.S. trade promotion by providing funds for feasibility studies, market surveys and what are called "definitional missions." The purpose of the latter is to develop the information needed to make critical decisions about investing in projects overseas. These surveys and feasibility studies touch on virtually every business sector. Some recent examples include a survey of potential mining and natural resource development projects in Nigeria; a feasibility study to build a second container terminal at the Port of Algiers; transportation infrastructure projects in Pakistan and the Philippines; and energy and power line development in Sri Lanka, Chile, and the Czech Republic.

This is an illustrative sampling of the initiatives USTDA has sponsored, the results of which are available free of charge in USTDA's on-line reference library. Recent projects USTDA has commissioned, and information on how to compete for new projects is available on the website www.ustda.gov.

# THE MILLENNIUM CHALLENGE
# CORPORATION (MCC)

The MCC (www.mcc.com) is a United States Government corporation created to provide assistance to developing countries who meet strict criteria of self-help, probity, and commitments to furthering the well-being of their population and to ending corruption. Established in January 2004, MCC has disbursed about $914.5 million in 39 countries around the world, with the majority in Africa and the Newly Independent States of the former Soviet Union. Before a country can become eligible to receive assistance, MCC looks at that country's performance on a range of political, economic and good governance criteria, and then selects eligible countries for the major bulk of its assistance. MCC funds, which are appropriated by the U.S. Congress every year, have financed projects in health and HIV/AIDS prevention and treatment; empowering women; food security; developing the private sector; water and sanitation; environment; democracy building; and infrastructure development.

## THE U.S. AGENCY FOR INTERNATIONAL DEVELOPMENT (USAID)

USAID (www.usaid.gov) is the primary source of assistance to developing countries and funds a broad range of programs and projects around the world that offer opportunities for the U.S. private sector, educational institutions and non-governmental organizations to provide goods and services internationally. With a budget of about $24.8 billion requested for fiscal year 2010, USAID targets assistance in five key areas: health, including HIV/AIDS prevention and treatment and maternal and child health; democracy-building and conflict prevention; economic growth and reform, agricultural development; infrastructure, especially water and sanitation; and emergency disaster relief and humanitarian missions.

Both MCC and USAID procurements can be found on-line at their websites, and at FedBizOpps. Export.gov provides a portal to all export-related assistance and market information offered by the federal government and provides trade leads, free export counseling, help with the export process, and more.

## GETTING HELP IN A FOREIGN COUNTRY

If you do run into problems in a foreign country, you can turn to the U.S. Embassy's Commercial Office for help. The Commercial Office can assist you by bringing U.S. Government support for your response to a tender in the host country, or helping you overcome obstacles in registering your company or product. This service is available through the U.S. Department of Commerce's Advocacy Center. Support can range from meetings by U.S. Commercial Officers with local officials or companies to letters and calls from high-level U.S. authorities, depending on the specific case needs.

Eligibility for the service and ground rules are listed at the www.buyusa website.

One important caveat: the U.S. Government will not advocate for one American company competing against another American company for an international contract, but only when an American company is competing against other foreign competitors.

It is important to initiate contact with the Advocacy Center, based in Washington, D.C., in the early stages of the project; requests usually take three to four weeks to be approved.

# GLOSSARY

## Bribe
Payment to someone in power or in the midst of negotiations to try to influence the outcome of a business deal. Considered illegal or at least unethical in most cultures, but there are some cultures that practice bribery as an accepted way of doing business.

## BRIC
An acronym for the countries of Brazil, Russia, India, and China, which are said by some to have expanding economies and so possess more business/job opportunities than other nations.

## Contract
A verbal or written agreement that spells out all the terms of a business deal; it is usually necessary for both parties to sign the agreement for it to be considered binding. Most contracts also spell out what resources will be available to either party if any terms of the contract are not enforced.

## Culture
The beliefs, values, attitudes, history, habits, food, dress, and language that is shared collectively by a people who usually live in the same geographic area; the orientation is still maintained despite relocation.

## Culture Shock
The reaction someone has when arriving in a place that has a culture that is dramatically different from the one that she or he is used to. Most Westerners will express culture shock when visiting India for the first time; they are less likely to feel that way when they visit England or Australia.

## EU

European Union started in the 1950s, with six nations, and now it has 27 European countries as members, united to make it easier to trade and work in any of those nations; 16 member states have adopted the use of the euro as their currency.

## Foreign Corrupt Practices Act (FCPA)

A U.S. law that makes it a crime for any United States citizen or company to offer, pay, transfer, or promise to pay or transfer, money or anything of value to get or keep business.

## Global

Another term for international; doing business beyond the borders of one's own country or continent.

## IP

Intellectual Property. Original information that is unique to an individual or a company that you seek to protect in doing dealings internationally so that no company sells or translates/sells that material (e.g., books; DVDs) or produces "knock-off" products (e.g., designer handbags) without consent or remuneration to the rightful IP owners.

## KSA

Abbreviation for Kingdom of Saudi Arabia.

## Local Agent

Individual who lives and works in the foreign country where business is being sought who acts on behalf of another party on a commission, salaried, or commission + salary basis.

## Non-Verbal Communication

The way that people speak without words by way of body posture, gestures and facial expressions; also the speed with which someone speaks; to convey emotion by way of kissing, hugging, or touching.

## Protocol

Expected behavior in a business setting. Varies from culture to culture, country to country. For example, whether or not an American president should bow to the royal family of Japan. Some use the term *protocol* interchangeably with *etiquette*.

## SEO

Search Engine Optimization. A way to increase the visibility of a website by having more search engines link to it through the key words that are associated with the site.

# BIBLIOGRAPHY

Asgary, Nader and Mark C. Mitschow. "Toward a Model for International Business Ethics." *Journal of Business Ethics*, Volume 36 (2002), pages 239-246.

Axtell, Roger. *Do's and Taboos Around the World*. 3rd edition. New York: Wiley, 1993.

Baldrige, Letitia. *Letitia Baldrige's Complete Guide to Executive Manners*. New York: Rawson Associates, 1985.

Barboza, David. "China Sentences Rio Tinto Employees in Bribe Case." *New York Times*, March 29, 2010, http://www.nytimes.com.

Bosrock, Mary Murray. *Put Your Best Foot Forward: Mexico, Canada*. St. Paul, MN: IES (International Education Systems), 1995.

Bryant, Adam. "Managing Globally, and Locally." Interview with Nancy McKinstry, CEO of Wolters Kluwer. *New York Times*, December 13, 2009, Business section, page 2.

Butler, Sue. *Culture Smart! New Zealand*. Portland, OR: Graphic Arts Center Publishing Company, 2006.

Caslione, John A. and Andrew R. Thomas. *Global Manifest Destiny*. Chicago: Dearborn Trade Publishing, 2002.

Carnegie, Dale. *How to Win Friends and Influence People*. New York: Pocket Books, 1936, 1940, 1964.

Curry, Jeffrey Edmund. *International Negotiating, 3rd edition*. Petaluma, California: World Trade Press, 2009.

DesChamps, Barbara. *It's in the Bag: The Complete Guide to Lightweight Travel*. CA: Chateau Publishing, 2003.

_____, *It's in the Bag: Your Custom Business and Travel Wardrobe*. CA: Chateau Publishing, 2007.

Delaney, Laurel. "How to Get Paid on International Transactions." Originally published at OPENForum.com. Reprinted at http://www.smallbiztrends.com on December 13, 2009.

Gamboa, Ernesto C. "How international is entrepreneurship?" *Entrepreneurship: Theory and Practice*, May 2008, pages 551-559.

Hall, Edward T. *The Dance of Life: The Other Dimension of Time*. Garden City, NY: Anchor Press/Doubleday, 1983.

*Harvard Business Review. Doing Business in China*. Cambridge, MA: Harvard Business School Publishing Corporation, 2004.

_____. "Managing Across Distance in Today's Economic Climate: The Value of Face-to-Face Communication." A report by *Harvard Business Review* analytic Services, Sponsored by British Airways, 2009.

Johnson, Dorothea. *The Little Book of Etiquette*. Philadelphia, PA: Running Press, 1997.

_____. *Tea & Etiquette: Taking Tea for Business and Pleasure*. Perryville, Kentucky: Benjamin Press, 2009.

Katz, Lothar. *Negotiating International Business*. Charleston, SC: BookSurge Publishing, 2nd edition, 2007.

Kooser, Amanda C. "Call of the World: Phone from Abroad." Posted at http://smallbusiness.aol.com, 12/12/2009.

Lander, Mark. "Europe Ponders the Meaning of Life." *The New York Times*, August 15, 2004, posted at www.nytimes.com.

Linkow, Peter R. "Managing Across Language, Culture, Time, and Location." New York: The Conference Board, 2008. 42 pages.

Malcolm, Andrew and Johanna Newman. "How low will he go? Obama gives Japan's Emperor Akihito a wow bow" *Los Angeles Times* blog, posted on November 14, 2009 (http://latimesblogs.latimes.com).

Mark, Elisabeth. *Breaking through Culture Shock*. London: Nicholas Brealey Publishing, 1999.

Martin, Jeanette S. and Lillian H. Chaney. *Global Business Etiquette*. Westport, CT: Praeger, 2006.

Milligan, Angela. *Customs & Etiquette of Australia*. London, UK: Simple Guides, Brava Ltd., 2007.

Mitchell, Charles. *International Business Ethics, 3rd edition*. Petaluma, California: World Trade Press, 2009.

Morrison, Terri, Wayne A. Conaway, and George A. Borden. *Kiss, Bow, or Shake Hands*. Holbrook, MA: Bob Adams, Inc., 1994.

"Number of Internet users worldwide reaches 2 bln: UN." Press release from the AFP (Agence France-Presse). Posted at Yahoo!® News, January 26, 2011.

O'Leary, Siobhan. "Publishing Expats: Working in France, Germany, Estonia and Ireland." January 13, 2010, http://www.publishing perspectives.com.

Pachter, Barbara and Margie Brody with Betsy Anderson. *Prentice Hall Complete Business Etiquette Handbook*. Englewood Cliffs, NJ: Prentice Hall, 1995.

Peddicord, Kathleen. *How to Retire Overseas*. New York: Hudson Street Press, 2010.

Ramsey, Lydia. "Shaking Hands throughout History and Around the World." http://workbloom.com, 2007.

Requejo, William Hernandez and John L. Graham. *Global Negotiation: The New Rules*. New York: Palgrave Macmillan, 2008.

Salacuse, Jeswald W. *The Global Negotiator*. New York: Palgrave Macmillan, 2003.

_____. *Making Global Deals*. Boston: Houghton Mifflin, 1991.

_____ ."Ten Ways that Culture Affects Negotiating Style: Some Survey Results." *Negotiation Journal*, July 1998, pages 221-240.

Shenkar, Oded. "One more time: international business in a global economy." *Journal of International Business Studies*, volume 35 (2004), pages 161-171.

Shippey, Karla C. *International Intellectual Property Rights, 3rd edition*. Petaluma, California: World Trade Press, 2009.

Smith, Huston. *The World's Religions*. Revised edition. New York: HarperOne, 1991, 1958.

Wilfong, James and Toni Seger. *Taking Your Business Global*. Franklin Lakes, NJ: Career Press, 1997.

Yager, Jan. *Business Protocol: How to Survive & Succeed in Business*. 1st edition published by Wiley, 1991. 2nd edition, Stamford, CT: Hannacroix Creek Books, Inc., 2001.

_____. "Business Protocol for Consultants." *Consultant News*, 10/91

_____ . *Effective Business and Nonfiction Writing, 2nd edition.* (New York, Arco, 1985, under the title *How to Write Like a Professional*; 2nd edition, Stamford, CT: Hannacroix Creek Books, Inc., 2001).

_____. "Holidays Offer Time to Cement Business Ties — or Sink Them." *Newsday*, December 8, 1991.

_____. "Mind Your Manners." *National Business Employment Weekly* cover story, Fall 1993.

_____. "Office Communications: Getting the Message Across." *Newsday*, April 4, 1988.

_____. "No Boundaries to Hatred." *New York Times Op-ed page,* January 12, 1974.

_____. *Productive Relationships: 57 Strategies for Building Stronger Business Connections.* Stamford, CT: Hannacroix Creek Books, Inc., 2011.

_____. "Something Inside Me Cried Out for India." *Times of India,* July 14, 1974.

_____. "Ten Unbecoming Ways to Get Yourself Kicked Out of Your Job." *Newsday,* Oct. 27, 1991.

_____. *Who's That Sitting at My Desk? Workship, Friendship, or Foe?* Stamford, CT: Hannacroix Creek Books, Inc., 2004.

# RESOURCES

## ASSOCIATIONS RELATED TO PROTOCOL, CROSS-CULTURAL TRAINING, NEGOTIATING, OR CORPORATE TRAVEL

Association of Image Consultants International (AICI)
www.aici.org
Educational and networking international association for those working in the image management field.

Association of Corporate Travel Executives (ACTE)
515. King Street, Suite 440
Alexandria, VA 22314
http://www.acte.org
Founded in 1988, a nonprofit education association with more than 6,000 members who are engaged in all aspects of corporate business travel in more than 80 countries.

Academy of International Business (AIB)
The Eli Broad College of Business
Michigan State University
7 Eppley Center
East Lansing, MI 48824-1121
http://aib.msu.edu
Founded in 1959, an association of scholars and experts in international business with more than 3,000 members in 81 countries.

## BUSINESS ETIQUETTE CONSULTANTS INCLUDING COMPANIES OFFERING CROSS-CULTURAL OR PROTOCOL TRAINING

Global Dynamics, Inc.
www.global-dynamics.com
Founded by sociologist Neal R. Goodman, Ph.D., this is a global company offering global training in "cultural intelligence" to men and women in corporations.

Negotiating Coach
955 South Virginia Street, Suite 116
Reno, Nevada 89502
9 Dooley Place
Guelph, Ontario Canada N1G 4M7
www.negotiatingcoach.com

Michael E. Sloopka, Founder
Michael@sloopka.com
Offers individual training and coaching as well as seminars on negotiation techniques.

My Negotiation Coach
1615 Old Hawkinsville Road
Dublin, GA. 31021
www.Mynegotiationcoach.com
Bill Adams and Wendy Kasulka will negotiate on your behalf or they will coach you to help you do the negotiating yourself.

## COUNTRY-BY-COUNTRY INFORMATION

Contact the local embassy or consulate to see what information they have about doing business with their country.

www.NegIntBiz.com

http://www.globalnegotiationresources.com/resources/countries/

Lothar Katz's website in which he provides free information on the 50 countries covered in his book, *Negotiating International Business*, with periodic updates at the website. Each country's write-up can be accessed individually and read online or downloaded as a PDF file.

Getting Through Customs

www.getcustoms.com

Website from the co-authors of the classic book on doing business in sixty countries, *Kiss, Bow, or Shake Hands* by Terri Morrison, Wayne A. Conaway, and George A. Borden, Ph.D. Offers selected free related articles, links to ordering the latest edition of their books, and information about their upcoming seminars.

Global Negotiation

www.globalnegotiationbook.com

Official website for William Hernandez Requejo and John L. Graham, co-authors of the book, *Global Negotiation: The New Rules*. Provides an excerpt of the book and a link to globalnegotationresources.com, with information on negotiating in fifty countries.

## ORGANIZATIONS OFFERING INFORMATION AND NETWORKING OPPORTUNITIES ON CONDUCTING BUSINESS

FCEM (Femmes Chefs d'Entreprises Mondiales)

World Association of Women Entrepreneurs

Forum Francophone des Affaires

3 Place de la Coupole BP98

Charenton 94223, CEDEX, France

http://www.fcem.org

Founded in France in 1945, membership organization of women entrepreneurs from around the world. Membership is through a national organization for women in business. In the United States, membership is through NAWBO (National Association of Women Business Owners).

World Chamber of Commerce
5588 Chamblee Rd. # 161
Dunwoody, Ga. 30338
info@worldchamberc.org
www.worldchamberc.org
Non-profit membership organization concerned with promoting international trade and investment.

## INTERNATIONAL FINANCIAL INSTITUTIONS

African Development Bank
www.afdb.org

Asian Development Bank
www.ADB.org

European Bank for Reconstruction and Development
www.ebrd.org

Inter American Development Bank
www.iadb.org

UN Development Business site
http://www.devbusiness.com

World Bank
www.worldbank.org

## CONVERSION TABLES

For shoe size
http://aglobalworld.com/internationalconversions/shoe

For clothing
www.the budgetfashionista.com/archive/internationalsizeconversion

For currency/money
www.xe.com

For time and date information around the world
www.timeanddate.com

## Acknowledgements

The list that follows offers my grateful acknowledgment to all who graciously gave me in-person or phone interviews during my three years of researching this book. Please note that any interviewees who requested anonymity are intentionally missing from this list. However, their contributions are not minimized by the concealment of their identities. I am also omitting from this list the more than two hundred additional men and women from around the world who answered my queries or filled out my 38-question international protocol and business confidential survey. (I also apologize in advance to anyone I unwittingly omitted.) Thanks to these individuals for their in-person or phone interview, or written communications: Professor Jeswald W. Salacuse; Henry J. Braker, Professor of Law at The Fletcher School of Law and Diplomacy, Tufts University, Medford, Massachusetts; Barry Petersen, Senior Correspondent, CBS News, Denver, Colorado; Neal R. Goodman, Ph.D., CEO Global Dynamics, Inc.; Rachna Kumar, Ph.D., Program Director, Business and Management Programs, Professor, Information Systems and Technology, Marshall Goldsmith School of Management, Alliant International University, San Diego, California; Rochelle Kopp, Japan Intercultural Consulting, Emerald Hills, California; Dan Poynter, international speaker and author; P. J. McGuire, Modet, Inc., Chicago, Illinois; William Melton, lawyer, New York, New York; Lindsay Adams, past president, Global Speakers Federation, CEO, Teamocracy, Brisbane, Australia; Nella Barkley, Co-Founder/CEO, Crystal Barkley; Ray Bowman, President, Bowman Business Services, Los Angeles, California; Leah D. Cochran; Alison Craig, President, 3 Impressions, Chicago, Illinois; Barbara DesChamps; Jan Diggs, General Manager, Business Development, Arabia Inform, Mohandiseen, Egypt; Peter Farina, President, ItalyMONDO! LLC, Italy; Lauren Gelman, journalist, Blurryedge.com; Eileen B. Hoffman, law school adjunct professor, Washington, D.C.; Kanak kr Jain; Diane DiResta, DiResta Communications, Inc., New York, New York; Judyt Mandel, international consultant, Washington, D.C.; Monica Marcel, Partner, Language & Culture Worldwide, LLC, Chicago, Illinois; Kay Maxwell, Executive Director, World Affairs Forum, Stamford, Connecticut; Rahul Mehandale, mySkin, Inc., New Jersey, with offices in Belgrade, Serbia and Pune, India; Adriana Navarro, Luminis, Madrid, Spain; Vered Neta, Amsterdam, Netherlands; Manikandan, External Communications, Manager, Dolcera, Hyderabad, India; Kathleen Peddicord, Founder, www.liveandinvest overseas.com; Murem Sharpe, CEO, Evoca LLC, Savannah, Georgia; Marilynn Smith, Ph.D., retired librarian; Abel Zalcberg, co-founder and CEO, OFM, Inc.; Thomas D. Zweifel, Ph.D., Senior consultant, Swiss consulting group, Zurich, Switzerland; Robyn Pearce, trainer and speaker, Auckland, New Zealand; Beverly and Pablo Solomon, Austin, Texas; and Solange Warner, Founder, World Chamber of Commerce.

# ABOUT THE AUTHOR

Jan Yager, Ph.D. is an international speaker, coach, sociologist, and the author of 30 books, translated into 25 languages, including the award-winning *Business Protocol*, which was chosen as a main selection by the Doubleday Bookspan Executive Book Club and has been translated into Spanish, Chinese, Vietnamese, and Russian. Dr. Yager's book, *When Friendship Hurts* (Simon & Schuster/Fireside Books), which includes a chapter on work and friendship, has been translated into 21 languages with four more translations in preparation. Other books include *Career Opportunities in the Publishing Industry* (Facts on File, Inc., 2nd edition, 2010); *Career Opportunities in the Film Industry* (Facts on File, Inc., 2nd edition, 2009); *Effective Business and Nonfiction Writing*, 2nd edition (Hannacroix Creek), *Productive Relationships* (Hannacroix Creek), *Work Less, Do More* (Sterling Publishing), *Friendshifts; 365 Daily Affirmations for Time Management*, and others.

Dr. Yager has been doing business internationally, and traveling for research for her writing projects as well as for business, including selling foreign rights to books into more than 28 languages, since her early twenties. She has a Ph.D. in sociology from The City University of New York, a Masters degree in criminal justice from Goddard College, and she did a year of graduate work in art therapy at Hahnemann Medical College. Dr. Yager has taught courses at several colleges and universities, most recently the University of Connecticut. She is a member of the National Speakers Association, the Global Speakers Federation, and AICI, the Association of Image Consultants International. For more on this author, go to: www.drjanyager.com

To book Dr. Yager as a speaker or workshop leader, contact your favorite speakers' bureau or write to her directly at: yagerinquiries2@aol.com.

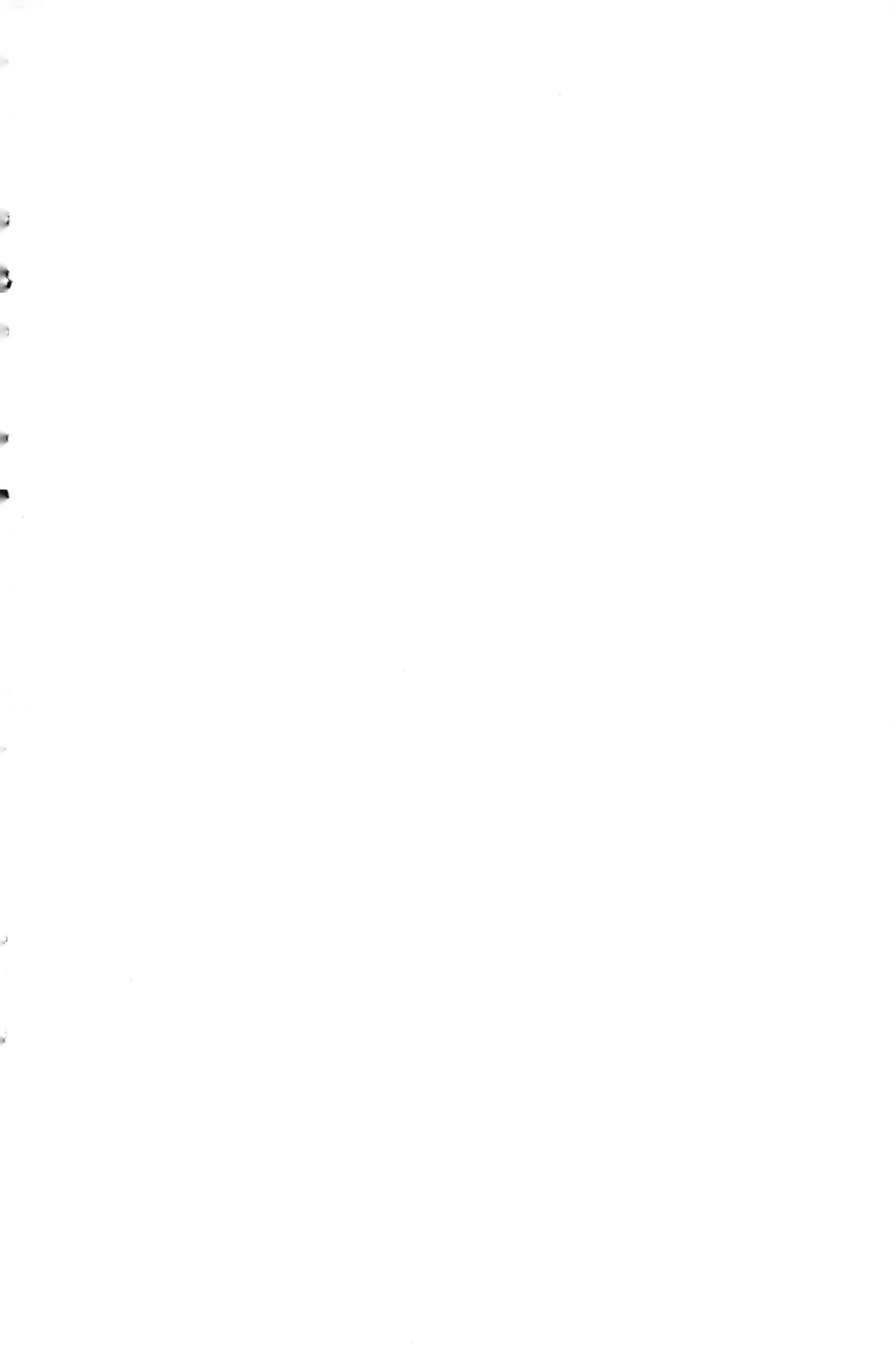

www.ingramcontent.com/pod-product-compliance
Lightning Source LLC
Chambersburg PA
CBHW021431180326
41458CB00001B/222